T0084758

Give Me Liberty

Other Titles of Interest from St. Augustine's Press

Gerhart Niemeyer, *The Loss and Recovery of Truth*

Gerhart Niemeyer, *Between Nothingness and Paradise*

St. Augustine, *On Order [De Ordine]*

Rémi Brague, *Eccentric Culture:*
A History of Western Civilization

Philippe Bénéton, *The Kingdom Suffereth Violence:*
The Machiavelli / Erasmus / More Correspondence
and Other Unpublished Documents

Joseph Cropsey, *On Humanity's Intensive Introspection*

Leo Strauss, *Xenophon's Socrates*

Leo Strauss, *Xenophon's Socratic Discourse*

James V. Schall, *The Regensburg Lecture*

James V. Schall, *The Modern Age*

Jacques Maritan, *Natural Law:*
Reflections on Theory and Practice

H.S. Gerdil, *The Anti-Emile:*
Reflectons on the Theory and Practice of Education
against the Principles of Rousseau

Andrew Pyle, ed., *Liberty:*
Contemporary Responses to John Stuart Mill

P. Armada, et al., eds., *Modernity and What Has Been Lost:*
Considerations on the Legacy of Leo Strauss

Karol Wojtyła [John Paul II], *Man in the Field of Responsibility*

Peter Kreeft, *Summa Philosophica*

Roger Scruton, *An Intelligent Persons Guide to Modern Culture*

Roger Kimball, *The Fortunes of Permanence:*
Culture and Anarchy in the Age of Amnesia

Paul M. Weyrich & William S. Lind, *The Next Conservatism*

Francis J. Beckwith, et al., eds., *A Second Look at First Things:*
A Case for Conservative Politics (Hadley Arkes Festschrift)

Give Me Liberty

Studies in Constitutionalism and Philosophy

by Ellis Sandoz

Eric Voegelin Society Studies

ST. AUGUSTINE PRESS

South Bend, Indiana

Copyright © 2013 by Ellis Sandoz

All rights reserved. No part of this book may be reproduced, stored in a retrieval system, or transmitted, in any form or by any means, electronic, mechanical, photocopying, recording, or otherwise, without the prior permission of St. Augustine's Press.

Manufactured in the United States of America

1 2 3 4 5 6   19 18 17 16 15 14 13

Library of Congress Cataloging in Publication Data
Sandoz, Ellis.
Give me liberty: studies in constitutionalism and philosophy / by Ellis Sandoz.
    pages cm. – (Eric Voegelin society studies)
Includes bibliographical references and index.
ISBN 978-1-58731-310-3 (pbk.: alk. paper) 1. Political science – United States – History. 2. Political science – Philosophy. 3. Liberalism – United States – History. 4. Constitutional history – United States. 5. United States – Politics and government. I. Title.
JA84.U5S25 2013
320.0973 – dc23   2013008874

∞ The paper used in this publication meets the minimum requirements of the American National Standard for Information Sciences Permanence of Paper for Printed Materials, ANSI Z39.481984.

ST. AUGUSTINE'S PRESS
www.staugustine.net

Mega biblion, mega kakon (Big book, big evil)

Callimachus (d. 240 B.C,.)

The Americans' love of freedom is the predominating feature which marks and distinguishes the whole. . . . This fierce spirit of liberty is stronger in the English colonies, probably, than in any other people on the earth. . . . The people are Protestants, and of that kind which is the most adverse to all implicit submission of mind and opinion. . . . [It] is a refinement on the principle of resistance: it is the dissidence of dissent, and the Protestantism of the Protestant religion . . . agreeing in nothing but in the communion of the spirit of liberty. . . . Slavery they can have anywhere. It is a weed that grows in every soil.

Edmund Burke, *Speech on Conciliation*

It was religion that gave birth to the English colonies in America. One must never forget that. In the United States religion is mingled with all the national customs and all those feelings which the word fatherland evokes. For that reason it has peculiar power. . . . Christianity itself is an established and irresistible fact which no one seeks to attack or to defend.

Alexis de Tocqueville, *Democracy in America*

Contents

Preface

This volume collects meditations exploring its announced subject, Give Me Liberty: Studies in Constitutionalism and Philosophy. The drift of them all is to show the connection of the individual consciousness with Liberty in persons and in polities as this has emerged in Western and endured in Anglo-American civilization. The philosophical intricacies of the relationships and their anchoring in the divine Ground of being is the theme of the later chapters. In the teeth of our witheringly secularist times, the argument raises the banner of human nobility through participation in the infinite Good as the foundation of all we hold dear and worthy of devotion now and throughout the preceding ages as we still remember them. Now as always before, resistance and conviction form the sine qua non of any Liberty worthy of the name. I hope that something of this spirit will find its way into the hearts and minds of my readers.

Ellis Sandoz
March 21, 2012

Acknowledgments

I herewith acknowledge with thanks kind permission to copyright holders to include herein in revised form two of my previously published essays:

"Religion and the American Founding." *Regent University Law Review* 20, no. 1 (2007–2008): 17-30. Copyright © 2007 Regent University Law Review.

"The Philosopher's Vocation: The Voegelinian Paradigm." *Review of Politics* 71 (2009): 54–67. © University of Notre Dame; reprinted in Catherine H. Zuckert, ed., *Political Philosophy in the Twentieth Century: Authors and Arguments* (Cambridge: Cambridge University Press, 2011), 80–90. Copyright © 2011 Cambridge University Press.

I also wish to thank my graduate student Sarah Beth Vosburg for fine editorial assistance in preparing the text; Julie Schorfheide for expert copy-editing of the typescript; Linda Webster for preparation of the index; my eldest son Ellis Sandoz III for preparation of promotional material; and Bruce Fingerhut, publisher, for his heartening support in bringing the book to publication in a timely fashion. Whatever the book's shortcomings, they are, of course, my own.

1. The Free Man and the Free Government in Political Philosophy

The Sabbath was made for man, and not man for the Sabbath.
Mark 2:27

Liberal modern constitutionalism on the Anglo-American pattern posits free men as citizens and free governments resting on consent of the governed. This magnification of the individual human person in his political capacity is both commonplace and unique – commonplace to our thinking and unique in world experience. My purpose here is briefly to explore the depth of meaning inherent in these political symbols and their theoretical grounding. To that end I shall consider the anthropology of liberty and something of its institutional manifestations. This will involve a certain amount of archeology, but my intention is to recall intimations of the living truth of our core convictions and their infrastructure as they coalesced in the Founding and to discern some hints as to their meanings. At the center of it all, viewed from philosophy and from revelation, stands the individual person living in the presence of divine Reality. How is this to be understood?

1. A Constitutional Preamble

To begin in the middle – i.e., with the political and constitutional layer of metaxic, or "In-Between," reality – there is the *liber homo* of Magna Carta, a primary beneficiary of some of the key provisions of that most celebrated constitutional document. Most famously there is cap. 29 (originally cap. 39):

> No Free-man [*Nullus liber homo*] shall be taken, or imprisoned, or dispossessed, of his free tenement, or liberties, or

free customs, or be outlawed, or exiled, or in anyway destroyed; nor will we condemn him, nor will we commit him to prison, excepting by the legal judgment of his peers, or by the laws of the land [*per legem terre*]. – To none will we sell, to none will we deny, to none will we delay right or justice.[1]

We can rightly join Sir Edward Coke, from his perspective in the seventeenth century, in seeing this and related passages of Magna Carta as forming the cornerstone of individual liberty in the Anglo-American constitutional tradition of rule of law with jury trial as an essential validating and enforcement mechanism. These developments were evident already in the fourteenth century: Parliamentary enactment of six laws between 1331 and 1368 interpreted "lawful judgment of peers" to mean trial by jury and the phrase "law of the land" to mean "due process of law," and expanded "no free man" to include all men *equally* by first rendering it "no man" and then "no man of whatever estate or condition he may be."[2] In the habit of the common law mind, all of this, and the Great Charter itself, was seen as confirmation of immemorial law and not innovation, in unchanging effect, since the memory of man runneth not to the contrary, as Sir John Fortescue quaintly said and Coke repeated.

In the 1460s, Fortescue, Lord Chief Justice and briefly Chancellor of England, elaborates the constitutional implications for a mixed monarchy that he calls *regimen politicum et regale,* a political and royal regime, one that secures liberty under law by parliamentary restraint of the monarch.[3] English laws, Fortescue never tires of insisting, are based on consent, in contrast to the *lex regia* of the civil law of France, by which whatever pleases the

1. Ellis Sandoz, ed., *The Roots of Liberty: Magna Carta, Ancient Constitution, and the Anglo-American Tradition of Rule of Law,* (1993; repr. Indianapolis: Liberty Fund / Amagi Books, 2007), 340, 347–48.
2. Quoting J. C. Holt, *Magna Carta,* 2nd ed. (1964; repr. Cambridge: Cambridge University Press, 1992), 10.
3. Sir John Fortescue, *On the Laws and Governance of England,* ed. Shelley Lockwood (Cambridge: Cambridge University Press, 1997), 20–23 (*Praise,* chap. 13), 83–90 (*Governance,* chaps. 1–3).

prince has the force of law and, consequently, where tyranny masquerades as monarchy. English laws guarantee liberty along with an array of individual rights very much the same as those claimed 300 years later in the American Declaration of Independence and assured by the Bill of Rights of 1791. Echoing Magna Carta, Fortescue mentions jury trial, a required plurality of witnesses, security against billeting troops in private houses, payment for lodging them in public establishments, security of private property against arbitrary invasion or taking, no legal use of torture to extract confessions, no taxation or changing of the law except with parliamentary assent. The common lawyer's devotion to immemoriality and appeal to the past as precedent (*stare decisis*) thereby to fashion a historical jurisprudence is transformed before our eyes, as it were, into a natural law jurisprudence that Englishes that of Fortescue's master, Saint Thomas Aquinas. The mixed republic of the ancient Israelites that he so admired is declared by Fortescue, in his *In Praise of the Laws of England,* to be the very model for the English monarchy itself. Centuries later, Lord Acton enthusiastically recognized Aquinas as the first Whig for his part in this discovery as it embraced mixed monarchy like that in England as the best *practicable* form of government.

However that may be, what we familiarly call "free government" itself was theorized in the process, became a living force in the land in the turbulent passage from Tudor rule to Glorious Revolution, and taught Englishmen in America the lessons of liberty under law they put to the test in the Founding. John Locke had reminded readers of the noble principle of the *consent* essential to free government as laid down by the judicious Richard Hooker and taken to heart in America: "Laws they are not which public approbation hath not made so."[4] The barons at Runnymede had sought a restoration of their *property* and insisted that scutages and aids could only be levied by *consent,* to be given by mustering, in that pre-parliamentary era, all the tenants-in-chief of the Crown – but this was already customary practice

4. John Locke, *Second Treatise of Civil Government* §134, quoting Richard
    Hooker, *Of the Laws of Ecclesiastical Polity,* bk. 1, chaps. 10.8–9.

even by then. Edmund Burke would later say that *liberty* is no abstract thing but "inheres in some sensible object." In England it had always related to taxing, and he recognized the authentic genealogy in the colonists' plea for "no taxation without representation."[5] Americans accepted from Fortescue and elsewhere the blend of common-law constitutionalism and natural-law teaching some thought inimical to it: Liberty was instilled into human nature by the hand of the Creator Himself, he taught. The laws of nature and nature's God in the Declaration of Independence thus implied not merely *duties* but correlative inalienable *rights* as well, as Algernon Sidney had already argued a century earlier.[6] With these rights and duties came a stubborn vision of free men living in brotherhood under free government as thereby according with divine Providence itself. Constitutionally and legally, it was said, under such a regime it was far better that twenty guilty men go free than for one innocent man to be punished wrongly.[7]

As the debate in America intensified after passage of the Declaratory Act, the blend of Coke, Locke, and natural law can be seen in John Adams's claim: "Rights antecedent to all earthly government – Rights that cannot be repealed or restrained by human laws – Rights derived from the great Legislator of the universe. . . . British liberties are not the grants of princes or parliaments, but original rights, conditions of original contracts . . . coeval with governments." And elsewhere it was asserted "that it is an essential, unalterable right, in nature, engrafted into the British constitution, as a fundamental law, and ever held sacred and irrevocable . . . that what a man has honestly acquired is absolutely his own, which he may freely give, but [which] cannot

---

5. Burke, *Speech on Conciliation with America*, March 1775; cf. Ellis Sandoz, *A Government of Laws: Political Theory, Religion, and the American Founding* (1990; repr. Columbia: University of Missouri Press, 2001), 164–65.

6. Algernon Sidney, *Discourses Concerning Government*, ed. Thomas G. West (Indianapolis: Liberty Fund, 1996), 406.

7. In Fortescue's phrasing: "I should, indeed, prefer twenty guilty men to escape death through mercy, than one innocent to be condemned unjustly." *On the Laws and Governance of England*, 41 (*Praise*, chap. 27).

be taken from him without his consent."[8] At the First Continental Congress in 1774, George Washington did not need to consult Locke to express his resolve never to submit "to the loss of those valuable rights and privileges, which are essential to the happiness of every free State, and without which life, liberty, and property are rendered totally insecure."[9] This was by then the settled common sense of the subject.

2. Libretto and Music

The experiential and theoretical grounding of free government as institutionalized in our constitutional order lies in historical tradition and long political practice as shaped especially by Hellenic noesis (much of it mediated by Cicero) and biblical revelation, i.e., by philosophy and Christianity. Thus, Sir Lewis Namier contends that "what matters most about political ideas is the underlying emotions, the music to which the ideas are mere libretto, often of very inferior quality."[10] We may have just been hearing noble strains of this music, and something like it also is evidenced in Patrick Henry's famous cry, "Give me liberty or give me death!" – plainly no syllogism. But the partition is artificial and all dichotomies suspect. The analytical and doctrinal abstractions arising from noetic insight and pneumatic vision can be discerned as a kind of desiccated postmortem autopsy report on human experience; but of themselves, they have little vitality or persistence when cut off from the engendering living truth they coolly articulate, any more than the technical notation of the score gives you the composer's melody. Again, we are in the middle, the preeminently human *metaxy,* or In-Between reality of experience,

8. Quoted by Edward S. Corwin, *The "Higher Law" Background of American Constitutional Law* (Indianapolis: Liberty Fund / Amagi Books, 2008), 74–75.
9. Letter of Washington to Capt. Robert McKenzie, Oct. 9, 1774, in *Writings of George Washington,* ed. W. C. Ford, 14 vols. (London and New York: G.P. Putnam, 1889), vol. 2.
10. Namier, "Tales from Arabia," *The Economist,* June 24, 2006, 11.

standing astride the thing itself taken to be cognizable and true and our symbolic representations of it in words, images, definitions, and assorted tools of knowing. From the perspective of human affairs it is consciousness that does this work, namely, the concrete consciousness of some individual person – a Plato, Augustine, or Aquinas, for instance – and bids us to look and see if this is not the case. The In-Between (*metaxy*) as the participatory sphere of human striving in politics is itself such an experience-symbol, representing the before and after of reflection, the birth and death of the individual's life span, the beginning and end of creation, and within that expanse of unfolding history, the height and depth of the cosmos, from the mysterious *apeiron,* or unbounded of Anaximander, to the articulate Nous as the Third God in Plato, for instance (*Laws* 712e–714a). The institutional residue of a mature political tradition forming the habits of liberty and justice in a citizenry, and preserving it through routine operations of government, is the prudential triumph of the music of man's experience of order in reality.

This flotsam and jetsam of the contemplative lives of individual human beings – the spiritual virtuosi of millennial stature, who illumine mankind's understanding of our common reality – includes also representations of political existence in terms of the individual human person. The *polis is MAN writ large,* Socrates playfully taught in the *Republic.* The model of the polity is the psyche of the individual human being, its order and disorders that of the souls of its citizenry, the constitution the soul of society, the soul the constitution of the man, and so on. This is called the anthropological principle, elaborated by the old Greeks as an enduring primary interpretive insight into the structure of political reality. Side by side with this comes the obvious question: But whatever is a Man? He is the self-reflective part of being, In-Between reality bridging the distance from the animals to God and partaking of both in a most disconcerting and inconvenient manner. Kierkegaard's dour comment comes to mind: Man is created a little lower than the angels, yet more often than not lives like his dog. Thus man, despite all mutilations and waywardness, is ineluctably *theomorphic*. He must have a true theology before he can have a true account of himself or be condemned by his own obtuseness or rebelliousness to live a lie, Plato argued – the *alethes pseudos,* or True Lie, as Socrates called the ignorance of the soul about being (*Republic* 382a–b).

Analytically the old Greeks, as you remember, elaborated a tri-partite model of the soul – reason, passions, and something in between these difficult to discern and called spiritedness or heart (*thymos*), the ally of hegemonic reason in constraining obstreper-ous passion or the appetites and helping to govern it in individual conduct, so that we do the right thing even when tempted to act unjustly or libidinously. The virtuous or good man manifested wisdom, courage, and temperance in a stable equilibrium orient-ed toward the transcendent Good and, thereby, was said to be just in himself. The vision of *Agathon*, or infinite Good "beyond" all finite goods and being itself, experientially forms the soul of the spiritually responsive person so that participation in the divine animates his life and enlivens the derivative lesser goods and per-sonal excellences identified as various virtues – of which Aristotle made a lengthy catalog for our guidance. He forever stressed that not knowing but *doing* is the core of prudential science, that we know the philosopher or mature or prudential man (*spoudaios* or *phronimos*) through exemplification rather than definition – the incarnation of goodness as *arete* or excellence, as the fulfillment of human potential in actual life. Such a life of mind, character, and existence will be happy and, if graced by the divine Reality, blessed (*makarios*), discernible in the contemplative's life of quest-ing openness partaking of the divine as a process of immortalizing (*athanatizein*) whose happiness rises far above that attained through the other excellences of character and mind (*Nicomachean Ethics* 10.7–8 1177a13–1178a8). Philosophy itself may then be emblemized as the imitation of Socrates, just as Christianity is the imitation of Christ. With the intervention of *revelation* the love of wisdom exemplary in antiquity takes on new meaning to become the questing soul's *fides quaerens intellectum,* or faith in search of understanding, in the *Proslogion* of Anselm of Canterbury (d. 1109), the founder of medieval Christian philosophy. Once you are in possession of revelation, Étienne Gilson asks, "how can you possibly philosophize as though you had never heard of it?"[11] The question remains.

These processes all lie within the existential sphere of the *individual* human being concretely considered to be the pre-eminent human reality, a view taken also by Thomas Aquinas in his *Summa contra gentiles* (3.2.113). So far from being a merely mortal or a Lockean possessive individual, or much less a Marxian nodal point gathering in the sum total of social relationships, the human person's distinction is that he alone partakes of immortality and is "capable of God," as John Wesley insisted, following Hooker. The human person finds his perfection (happiness, felicity, beatitude) in communion with the divine Reality in which he participates and by which he is constantly formed and nurtured. Not merely is the materialist reduction rejected, but *spiritual* individualism persuasively emerges as the true human *differentia specifica* and the crown of personal openness to the ineffable transcendent. The Christian vision of sojourner man as potentially *imago Dei* augments the Greek philosophical analysis. Augustine's trinitarian anthropology elaborates the insight in a memorable passage:

> We indeed recognize in ourselves the image of God . . . [one which] is yet nearer to Him in nature than any other of His works, and is destined to be yet restored, that it may bear a still closer resemblance. For we both are and know that we are, and delight in our being, and our knowledge of it. . . . I am most certain that I am, and that I know and delight in this. . . . For, as I know that I am, so I know this also, that I know. And when I love these two things I add to them a certain third thing, namely, my love, which is of equal moment. . . . Further, as there is no one who does not wish to be happy, so there is no one who does not wish to be. For how can he be happy, if he is nothing? (*City of God* 11.26)

11. Gilson, *The Spirit of Medieval Philosophy*, trans. A. H. C. Downes (New York: Charles Scribners' Sons, 1940), 5.

Faith and reason thus experientially fashion a mutually reinforcing texture supporting man's – *every* man's – differentiated tensional existence under divine presence and our understanding of the human condition itself. These classical and Christian perspectives on human existence were familiar and fully propagated in mid-eighteenth-century America through the sermons attended by the generality of the population and in the colleges attended by those destined for leadership in the country. The revivals, in effect, moved personal meditation and prayer from the internal forum to the open public forums of congregations and assemblies in the streets and fields. There auditors were exhorted to move by individual decision and continual perseverance from ruin to restoration – as Augustine had sketched the dynamic of human destiny – going on to perfection as *New Men* by accepting the call of Christ's saving grace through faith (Matt. 5:48; Eph. 4:22–24). While the golden age of the classics reigned in academe, the Bible was the university of the general populace. One scholar (Sidney Mead) even concludes that America is a nation with the soul of a church.

3. The Captain of My Ship

There remains in all of this an untidy ambiguity to be addressed, if not resolved. The rugged individualist imagines himself to be the captain of his ship and the master of his fate. True to a point, taken absolutely this becomes egophany and narcissistic rebellion against the divine ground as understood in both philosophy and faith, by Eric Voegelin's analysis. For all of his grandeur and nobility, the individual human being's dignity is limited by his place in the hierarchy of being, in the comprehending reality of which he is uniquely a self-reflective participant. The limitation is signaled in many ways – by his ineluctable mortality emphatically, and symbolized as well in the Creator-creaturely relationship announced to all in the Declaration of Independence and in Locke's insistence that we are not wholly our own property but also God's – as Genesis originally said and Aquinas affirmed

(Locke, *Second Treatise* §6; Aquinas, *Summa theologica* I–II, q.94, a.5). The "autonomous Man" claim (positivist, Marxian, Nietzschean, fascist, or liberal) that so bedevils modernity is a libidinous deformation of the truth of being and a fallacious occlusion of reality, the *hubris* of antiquity and very *superbia vitae* that animates the contemporary rebellion of ideologues of all stripes. It implies or directly asserts the death of God. The ego-phanic rebellion itself, despite its pretensions to the contrary, can only be propagated through the very destruction of personhood, of man in the name of man with which we are painfully familiar. The reduction of human beings to atomized individuals bereft of attachment to God or love of their fellow men thereby makes of them suitable material for the building of socialism or for effectu-ating the Nazi utopia (Hannah Arendt) or other mass movements fulfilling the totalitarian impulse. The true "rugged individual" of our tradition and ontology, on the other hand, is anchored in com-monsense reality while acknowledging his own human *inability* as nobility enough for a person engaged in the divine-human collab-oration whereby the ineffable becomes effable in biography, histo-ry, and human affairs, an intimation of divine Providence. Thus, he serves – each on his own in unique ways – as an under-work-man in the vineyard of liberty, as John Adams remarked. This role was glory enough even for that crusty old Argonaut on his jour-ney through time in partnership with God with his resolute band of brothers.

This view implies a further limitation of the individual, which is at the same time also a liberation: He is naturally political, to accept Aristotle's argument – and to qualify the textbook account of Locke's; and by reason of his moral sense he lives in communi-ties grounded in agreement about good and evil, right and wrong, justice and injustice. Whether this *moral sense* (the Greek *storgé*) is merely natural or is "infused" into the soul by God was part of the heated debate in the eighteenth century between Francis Hutcheson and Jonathan Edwards as well as John Wesley and John Witherspoon, but its presence and centrality as a defining human trait were acknowledged on both sides. It provides the foundation of association and free government in *homonoia,* or like-mindedness, whereby persuasion can succeed at least some of the time in fostering agreement to rational policy and just law – thereby allowing God and reason alone to rule through consent, to the extent that may be practicable in fractious human affairs. The person is *freest* when he serves truth and justice and does not live his life enslaved to error or vice, our sources persuasively argue. The possibility of a "government of laws and not men" implied such an anthropology when Aristotle first elaborated it. That same anthropology was woven into the fabric of the U.S. Constitution by the Founders in pitting the reason of the law against the passion of the human governors as they incorporated institutional self-equilibrating checks and balances into its normal operational processes. They thereby sought to foster institutionally liberty and just dominion grounded in consent – beginning from the sober assumption that government is itself the greatest of all reflections on human nature, a true masterstroke.

4. The Politics of Aspiration

The notions of free and responsible individuals and of *liberty* as the cardinal good underlying free government and the market economy must be contextualized roughly along lines I have indicated in part 1 to be fully persuasive representations of the American Founders' consensus. Ours is a politics of *aspiration* – it is devoted to "the pursuit of happiness" – by inheritance, tradition, and rational conviction.[12] Self-love and love of God are not in Manichaean (Gnostic) opposition to one another or they could never have been brought together to form the Great Commandment and its corollary, a delicate matter to be sure (Matt. 22:37–39). This aspiring openness is more than merely an Anglo-American prejudice. It goes to the root of our civilization. And we need to remind ourselves that the universal appears only

---

12. Henri Bergson's term in *Two Sources of Morality and Religion*; see the discussion in Sandoz, *A Government of Laws*, 48–49.

in particulars as their exemplifications. The broil of scorched-earth, interest-based politics and raw self-centered ethics may serve the material well-being of free societies, but – vital as they are for securing economic vigor and the free market against the radical collectivizers and secularizers of our time – *there is more!* They *alone* do not and cannot suffice for the politics of aspiration central to our ontology and our institutions and their ultimate foundations. They have been and must be held in check by our abiding theoretical principles, habits, and institutions expressive of a sound anthropology or "true map of man," as John Adams called it.[13]

What then? Aspiration to what? *Good.* This less-than-startling answer is the one that has been offered since Plato, one amplified and democratized over the millennia. It forms the core of our own civilization and remains the enduring center of personal, historical, and ontological order. Infatuated with novelty as we are, I wish the truth seemed less tedious and the answer about it less predictable. But perhaps unoriginality is the mark of truth in human affairs. In any event, this answer best accommodates the politics of free men and free governments open to creativity and human flourishing. As John Dickinson famously insisted in the Federal Convention, "Experience must be our only guide. Reason may mislead us." The foundation is judgment informed by common sense.

From his perspective in the same century with which we began, that of Magna Carta, Thomas Aquinas theorized the ancient Greek insight that all things aim at the Good as the foundation of moral natural law and politics. This is the self-evident first principle of the practical reason he taught. It is arguably still self-evident, if anything is, even in our own discordant age. The logic is driven by its empirical appeal to reflective experience: Look and see if this is not the case, Thomas in effect asks. It is *love* (as inclination) that drives the analysis guided by reason – for

13. See the discussion in Sandoz, *Republicanism, Religion, and the Soul of America* (Columbia: University of Missouri Press, 2006), chap. 1, §8.

ourselves and self-preservation most immediately, then for propagation of children, their education and familial well-being, and lastly for what is most properly human, viz. knowledge of the truth about God (*summum bonum*) and the terms of living together in discrete polities (*ST* I–II, q.94, a.2). The ontological and axiological ascent brings to mind the insight of the meditatives and mystics – themselves spiritual individualists – that all love is a love of God, even when most unaware of itself. These glories largely lie beyond our immediate concerns here, although never entirely: The biological man is also the economic, political, intellectual, and spiritual man simultaneously in every instance and every moment of life. It is important to notice that the experiential orientation disclosed by the First Epistle of John, chapter four, which proclaims that "God is love" and that "we love Him because He first loved us" (verses 8 and 19), underlies much that is centrally relevant and immediately intelligible to any Bible reader. These readers included most of the population of America at the time of the Founding, especially when the matter is considered against the backdrop of the Great Awakening and its enduring effects. It also had inspired the great philosophy of man elaborated by Aquinas in terms of *fides caritate formata* as grounded in *amicitia,* which is arguably the culmination of Scholastic philosophy (*SCG* 3.2.91 149–51). A comparable understanding of spiritual reality cannot be discounted as foreign to leading Protestant Americans and to the evangelists of our time period (such as Jonathan Edwards, Ezra Stiles, John Witherspoon, and John Wesley's Methodist missionaries), as I have attempted to show more fully elsewhere.

However: To be stressed at the same time is the fact that the human pilgrimage is lived in the In-Between, or metaxic reality, where politics and economics ineluctably and rightly command great attention. The pursuit of worthy lesser goods than the transcendent Good need not involve the stark contrast originally envisaged by Augustine (*Civitas Dei* 14.28) – Aquinas conceded and the British moral and common sense philosophers insisted and persuasively argued. *Amor habendi* turns out to have a silver lining after all. As the sage Josh Billings neatly summarized things,

"Most of the happiness in this world consists of possessing what others can't get." Private property, long experience convinces us, is central to human liberty and personal fulfillment in our tradition, as was clear in Magna Carta, in Burke's insistence on tangibility, and as Aristotle contended against Socrates in the *Politics* (1262b22–25, 1263b1–4) when he said: "There are two motives that most cause men to care for things and be fond of them, the sense of ownership and the sense of preciousness. . . . [T]o feel that a thing is one's private property makes an inexpressibly great difference in one's pleasure; for the universal feeling of love for oneself is surely not purposeless but a natural instinct." Moreover, human *dominion* over the earth as showing man's political nature and vocation is tied to property and its sanctity – and to the individual bearing his own arms as the mark of a free man – in limiting government's reach, the Founders vociferously argued. To add John Witherspoon's voice, that of the most influential professor in American history: "If we take tradition or Revelation for our guide, the matter is plain, that God made man lord of the works of his hands, and puts under him all the other creatures. . . . Private property is every particular person's having a confessed and exclusive right to a certain portion of the goods which serve for the support and conveniency of life." "There is not a single instance in history in which civil liberty was lost, and religious liberty preserved entire. If therefore we yield up our temporal property, we at the same time deliver the conscience into bondage."[14] From this influential perspective, self-love is ameliorated by benevolence in every human breast (whether naturally or by divine infusion); the energetic competition for scarce goods, including honors and wealth, among free men not merely yields individual prosperity but inadvertently also serves the common good of the whole of society – "the greatest happiness for the greatest numbers." Passionate, competitive, even tumultuous, conflict among individuals and groups seems subtly guided by Jupiter's "invisible hand" in the guise of Providential purpose,

---

14. See Sandoz, *A Government of Laws*, 214.

further evidence of the inscrutable role of divine grace in human affairs, one more mysterious illustration of *felix culpa*. And thereby did God and Mammon finally sweetly kiss in America. Worldly success thus betokens divine favor and, seen soteriologically, is perhaps a cheerful augury strengthening hope for election and eternal salvation.

5. Conversion, Homonoia, and *Salus Populi*

We now must briefly consider these key issues, however inadequately. Alexis de Tocqueville grappled with related problems in studying the place of religion in American life in the 1830s and in seeking to explain individualism and self-interest rightly understood. In addition to the happy relation between making money and serving God that he thought so striking, what he found "unprecedented" was the spectacle of a society converted to the truth of the transcendent Good apparently reserved by the classic philosophers for the few. As one scholar has recently observed:

> America, from that view, is evidence that the Christians are right and the classical philosophers wrong about the human soul: Most human beings do not live trapped in some political "cave" oblivious to the truth . . . the Americans all display the spiritual restlessness that the aristocrats believed was possible for only a few. Tocqueville writes "it was necessary that Jesus Christ come to earth to make it understood that members of the human species are naturally alike and equal." And that's because "The most profound and vast geniuses of Rome and Greece were never able to arrive at [that] idea."[15]

The comparability or *equivalence* of the turn of the individual man from error (ignorance, *doxa*, sin) toward transcendent truth symbolized in Plato's *periagoge* in the Allegory of the Cave and

---

15. Kenneth L. Deutsch and Joseph R. Fornieri, *An Invitation to Political Thought* (N.p.: Cengage Learning, 2009), 413; Tocqueville, *Democracy in America*, 2.1.3.

in Christ's *metanoia* in the Gospel (Matt. 4:17), both representing crucial conversion experiences, is readily conceded. This complex subject cannot detain us here beyond the acknowledgment,
and further general agreement, that the implication of human
equality is indeed more pronounced in the Christian horizon, as
Tocqueville says – although it is by far not absent from Plato and
Aristotle: What makes a human being is equal possession of a
common nature by all such beings, whatever the scope, variety,
and degrees of actualization in individual cases and the empirical
evidence of slaves by nature; the Pamphylian myth that concludes
the *Republic* (614b) is the tale of everyman. But that Christ came
to all, not merely to some elite, is the unequivocal point. (John
10:9–10). Thus to be stressed is that the biblical "*metanoia* is the
human act of penitence *and* the divine act of salvation; it is both
a human task and a divine gift."[16] This divine-human collabora-
tion is clearly recognized philosophically in Jonathan Edward's
Christian neo-Platonism and elsewhere. And more than this:
Christ is present to all human beings as their substance and inde-
structible dignity, the chief burden of Matthew 25:40, 45:
"Inasmuch as you have done it unto one of the least of these, my
brethren, you have done it unto me." The assurance of equality
and the brotherhood of man in diversity of talents is already the
teaching of Plato's Phoenician tale (myth of the metals, *Republic*
414c). That insight is amplified in the Apostle Paul's powerful
account of the divine charismata apportioned to every person by
God as participants in the mystical Body of Christ (1 Cor. 12).
The culmination of these differentiations of *human equality*
under the dispensation of grace comes with the glorious understanding of each faithful man as priest and king (1 Peter 2:9; Rev.
1:6).

The character of the political community freely binding
together individual men and women by consent and the necessity
that unites them may be noticed. If we begin from *homonoia*

16. Stefan Rossbach, *Gnostic Wars: The Cold War in the Context of a History
of Western Spirituality* (Edinburgh: University of Edinburgh Press, 1999),
41.

("concord"), as Aristotle termed the fundamental intellectual and spiritual consensus distinctive to human beings when organized into the *political* communities natural to them – a notion akin to the New Testament *isopsuchos* (translated as "like-minded" in KJV; see, e.g., Rom. 15:5), we find articulate identification of the core American unity from leading figures at the time of the Founding. Thus, in *Federalist No. 2* Publius (John Jay) wrote:

> Providence has been pleased to give this one connected country to one united people – a people descended from the same ancestors, speaking the same language, professing the same religion, attached to the same principles of government . . . who have nobly established their general liberty and independence . . . as if it was the design of Providence . . . an inheritance so proper and convenient for a band of brethren.

In justifying political union of this brotherhood under the Constitution, Publius (James Madison) later on appeals to the fundamental convictions of Americans: "to the great principle of self-preservation; to the transcendent law of nature and of nature's God, which declares that the safety and happiness of society are the object at which all political institutions aim and to which all such institutions must be sacrificed" (*Federalist No. 43*). Publius thus invokes Aristotle, Cicero, and the overarching principle of *salus populi* – as so often also had been done by John Selden, Sir Edward Coke, and the Whigs in the seventeenth-century constitutional debate. As Samuel Rutherford drolly phrased matters during the English civil war: "The law of the twelve tables is, *salus populi, suprema lex*. The safety of the people is the supreme and cardinal law to which all laws are to stoop" (*Lex, Rex* q.25). This was claimed as the ultimate ground of all free government and the basis for exercise of legitimate authority (not tyranny) over free men – the *liber homo* of Magna Carta and English common law. James Madison and the other Founders knew and accepted it as a fundamental of their own arduous endeavors and as an ineluctable requirement of true governance.

Decades later, John Adams, in a letter to Thomas Jefferson

(June 28, 1813), sought to recall the principled basis undergirding America's fragile cohesion during the Revolution and wrote:

> What were these *general Principles*? I answer the general Principles of Christianity, in which all those sects were united: And the *general Principles* of English and American Liberty, in which all those young Men United, and which had United all Parties in America, in Majorities sufficient to assert and maintain her Independence. Now I will avow, that I then believed, and now believe, that those general Principles of Christianity, are as eternal and immutable, as the Existence and Attributes of God; and those Principles of Liberty, are as unalterable as human Nature and our terrestrial, mundane System.[17]

6. Truth and Resistance to Untruth: Conclusion

The defiant fervor of the sentiments just remembered may be observed. Perry Miller once remarked that a cool rationalism such as Jefferson's might have declared the independence of such folk but could never have persuaded them to fight for it. This may be an injustice to Jefferson, but the larger point stands. Justice and truth lay at the heart of liberty as the Founders understood it to define the American cause – a cause assimilating all philosophy and revelation taught to propel a noble enterprise, one that helped change the world and still helps change it. Even in old age James Madison, last of the Founders, still admired the acuity of his generation in seeing the hand of tyranny in a three-penny tax on tea. If philosophy can be said to have been born in resistance to untruth in Hellenic antiquity, with untruth and injustice able to crush Athens's best man by legal decree, so also does statesmanship at its best serve truth and justice in those times of crisis that

---

17. *The Adams-Jefferson Letters: The Complete Correspondence Between Thomas Jefferson and Abigail and John Adams,* ed. Lester J. Cappon, 2 vols. in 1 (1959; repr. New York: Simon and Schuster, 1971), 2:339–40.

try men's souls. This is the practice of politics in an intellectual cosmion where "You shall know the truth, and the truth shall make you free" (John 8:32) is not merely slogan and shibboleth but words to live by. Aristotle's virtuous life as one of no regrets is nurtured by Paul's fighting the good fight and keeping the faith. Augustine's pronouncement that "an unjust law is no law at all" resonates as we read Plato's *Apology* and ponder his Socrates, and it fortifies every resistance to injustice since then, down to Martin Luther King's "Letter from Birmingham Jail" and our own civil rights revolution. As Eric Voegelin bluntly told the resplendent professorate and assembled studentry at the University of Munich, convened for his inaugural lecture there in 1958, many of whom had enjoyed promotion and prosperity from Hitler's largesse:

> The spiritual disorder of our time, the civilizational crisis of which everyone so readily speaks, does not by any means have to be borne as an inevitable fate; . . . on the contrary, everyone possesses the means of overcoming it in his own life. . . . No one is obliged to take part in the spiritual crisis of a society; on the contrary, everyone is obliged to avoid this folly and live his life in order.[18]

In sum, the individual person is free, and what he does counts in all spheres of endeavor. Everything in the history of the world was done by somebody. Adam sinned, and we all fall short of the glory of God. While we dutifully acknowledge the collective achievement of the Founders and capitalize the word in respect, Ralph Waldo Emerson was on to something when he suggested that all history is biography. A historian friend, in a moment of unguarded lucidity, opined that without George Washington and Abraham Lincoln there would be no United States of America. Another wrote: "Had James Madison never lived, the Constitution of the United States would probably not have been

18. Voegelin, *Science, Politics, and Gnosticism* (Wilmington, DE: ISI Books, 2004), 17; also in *Modernity Without Restraint*, ed. and intro. Manfred Henningsen (Columbia: University of Missouri Press, 2000), 261, vol. 5 of *The Collected Works of Eric Voegelin*, 34 vols.

written."[19] Alfred North Whitehead thought the whole history of philosophy merely a footnote to Plato. And we well may wonder what would have happened to Britain and our civilization without Winston Churchill, or how there could have been a Velvet Revolution without Ronald Reagan. Surely the butcher of Baghdad would still tyrannize Iraq but for George W. Bush.

So three cheers for the free man and the liberty we cherish! As we celebrate we remember our own favorite philosophers' considered sentiments: "Figure out what's right and go ahead," said Davy Crockett. "Work as though you'll live a hundred years, pray as though you'll die tomorrow," Poor Richard taught. And thereby you may achieve, Mark Twain hoped, "the serenity of a Christian holding four aces."

---

19. Jack N. Rakove, *The Beginnings of National Politics: An Interpretative History of the Continental Congress* (New York: Alfred A. Knopf, 1979), 468.

2. Religion and the American Founding

1. Introduction: Common Ground and General Principles – Recap of Basics

If we begin from *homonoia* ("concord"), as Aristotle termed[1] the fundamental intellectual and spiritual consensus distinctive to human beings when organized into the *political* communities natural to them – a notion akin to the New Testament *isopsuchos* (translated as "like-minded" in KJV; see, e.g., Rom. 15:5), we find articulate expression of core American unity from leading figures at the time of the Founding. Thus, in *Federalist No. 2* Publius (John Jay) wrote:

> Providence has been pleased to give this one connected country to one united people – a people descended from the same ancestors, speaking the same language, professing the same religion, attached to the same principles of government . . . who have nobly established their general liberty and independence . . . as if it was the design of Providence . . . an inheritance so proper and convenient for a band of brethren.[2]

In justifying political union of this brotherhood under the Constitution, Publius (James Madison) later on appeals to the fundamental convictions of Americans: "to the great principle of self-

---

1. "Concord [*homonoia*] . . . mean[s] friendship between citizens. . . . Now concord in this sense exists between good men, since these are of *one mind* both with themselves and with one another, as they always stand more or less on the same ground." Aristotle, *Nicomachean Ethics* 9.6.2–3, 1167b3–9, trans. H. Rackham, Loeb Classical Library (Cambridge, MA: Harvard University Press, 1975), 542–43. Italics added.
2. *Federalist No. 2* in *The Federalist Papers*, ed. Clinton Rossiter (New York: New American Library, 1961), 38.

preservation; to the transcendent law of nature and of nature's God, which declares that the safety and happiness of society are the object at which all political institutions aim and to which all such institutions must be sacrificed."[3] Publius thus invokes Aristotle, Cicero, and the overarching principle *salus populi, suprema lex esto* – as so often also had been done by John Selden, Sir Edward Coke, and the Whigs in the seventeenth-century constitutional debate. This was understood to be the ultimate ground of all free government and basis for exercise of legitimate authority (not tyranny) over free men – the *liber homo* of Magna Carta and English common law.[4] James Madison and the other Founders knew and accepted it as a fundamental of their own endeavors.

Decades later, John Adams, in a letter to Thomas Jefferson, remembered the principled basis of American cohesion during the Revolution:

> And what were these *general Principles*? I answer the general Principles of Christianity, in which all those sects were united: And the *general Principles* of English and American Liberty, in which all those young Men United, and which had United all Parties in America, in Majorities sufficient to assert and maintain her Independence. Now I will avow, that I then believed, and now believe, that those general Principles of Christianity, are as eternal and immutable, as the Existence and Attributes of God; and those Principles of Liberty, are as unalterable as human Nature and our terrestrial, mundane System.[5]

---

4. Cf. Samuel Rutherford, *Lex, Rex, or the Law and the Prince* . . . (1644; repr. Harrisonburg, VA: Sprinkle Publications, 1982), q. 25, p. 119: "The safety of the people is the supreme and cardinal law to which all laws are to stoop" – which he attributes to the Law of the Twelve Tables. For discussion, see Ellis Sandoz, *A Government of Laws: Political Theory, Religion, and the American Founding* (1990; repr. Columbia: University of Missouri Press, 2001), 116–18, 174, 197, 227. On "free man" in Magna Carta, see J. C. Holt, *Magna Carta*, 2nd ed. (1964; repr. Cambridge: Cambridge University Press, 1992), 9–11 and passim. See Cicero, *De legibus* 3.3.8.

5. John Adams to Thomas Jefferson, June 28, 1813, in *The Adams-Jefferson Letters: The Complete CorrespondenceBetween Thomas Jefferson and*

2. Elements of the Present Discussion

I. Structures and institutions: Notes on Virginia
II. Anthropology and ontology
III. Constitutional implications
IV. Postscript on freedom of conscience

I. Structures and institutions: Notes on Virginia

The true Christian is an *Englishman* and he is *free*![6] There is arrogant self-assurance in this conviction, obviously, but it seems to have been characteristic; and you may have noticed that politics is not a purely rational enterprise. Thus, Rev. William Crashaw's sermon to the Jamestown colonists in 1606 stated: "He that was the God of Israel is still the God of England." The attitude was commonplace, and in various forms it has persisted to define a central aspect of American "Exceptionalism."

Edward L. Bond writes of a pervasive sense of the "soteriology of empire" in the early years of Virginia. *Dominion* (Gen. 1:28; Ps. 8) over the land was based in the God-centered world of the time as a work done in *friendship* with the Creator. The form of the polity was intended to reflect that cardinal fact. This was a religious age "in which the ideas about God, the church, and religious devotion touched upon nearly all aspects of life, both public and private." Behavior rather than belief ruled the relationship to God in a Mosaic polity in which, in accordance with the Hebraizing

---

Abigail and John Adams, ed. Lester J. Cappon, 2 vols. in 1 (1959; repr. New York: Simon and Schuster, 1971), 2:339–40. For discussion, see Ellis Sandoz, *The Politics of Truth and Other Untimely Essays: The Crisis of Civic Consciousness* (Columbia: University of Missouri Press, 1999), 67–69.

6. "During the years of struggle against Catholicism and Spain, Englishmen were being conditioned to think of their country as specially elected to serve as a holy nation before the world. England's destiny under God – so a generation steeped in Foxe's *Book of Martyrs* agreed – was to spread the knowledge of divine truth, under God's providential care." Robert T. Handy, *A History of the Churches in the United States and Canada* (New York: Oxford University Press, 1977), 14.

Christianity then current in England, not primarily personal salvation but salvation through the dominion of a chosen nation on the Old Testament model prevailed. The English became the new elect or chosen people. The specific terms are given in the Virginia law code *Laws Divine, Morall and Martiall* (1610) that expressed English identity based on labor, worship, and Christian morality and followed the Ten Commandments.[7] Behavior took on "nearly sacramental character" to the neglect of the experiential *faith* essential to salvation, a defect Captain John Smith himself deplored at the time: "Our good deeds or bad, by faith in Christ's merits, is all we have to carry our souls to heaven or hell."[8]

Thus early on, the decisive existential *tension* toward transcendence clearly emerges that distinguishes between terrestrial and celestial empire, between the realms of caesar and of God. It structures all Western politics after Saint Augustine and is characteristic of Virginia's early years. The problematic is not tidy or simple, and its terms change with the times. But the *principle* remains: Human existence participates in all levels of reality but at all times must be lived in the *metaxy* or "In-Between" or middle-zone of time and eternity, mortality and immortality, of divine-human interaction. It abidingly limits earthly empires and human pretensions as a chastening, ineluctable dimension of reality itself. This is a cardinal insight of both philosophy and Christianity – one systematically subverted in the libidinous pretenses of all great tyrants (call them what you will) both religious and ideological, past and present – from the gnostic deformations of Boniface VIII to those of Karl Marx. Along the way America was born, asserting Liberty and justice in the face of perceived tyranny and raising the noble banner of a government of laws and not of men. In doing so it drew especially on the prudential

---

7. Quotations and interpretation from Edward L. Bond's account in *Damned Souls in Tobacco Country: Religion in Seventeenth-Century Virginia* (Macon, GA: Mercer University Press, 2000), 43–45, 50–51, 59–61, 66, 90, 129. See also Edward L. Bond, *Spreading the Gospel in Colonial Virginia: Preaching Religion and Community* (Lanham, MD: Lexington Books, 2005), passim.

8. Quoted from Bond, *Damned Souls,* 91.

science of human affairs created by Aristotle, who argued that "whoever asks the Law to rule asks God and Reason alone to rule; but he who asks a man to rule adds an element of the beast, for passion warps the minds of rulers even when they are the best of men. The Law [*nomos*] is reason [*nous*] unaffected by desire."[9]

In colonial Virginia, the Church of England was established by law. Thus, Bible, *Book of Common Prayer*, Apostles' Creed, Ten Commandments, and Sermon on the Mount supplied those "general principles of Christianity" John Adams later spoke of as grounding American consensus. Order depended on religion, and the core of worship was liturgical practice taken from the *Book of Common Prayer*. Of the settlers' routine, Captain John Smith tersely wrote: "Our order was daily to have Prayer, with a Psalm." Religious life was strictly maintained, with required attendance of morning and evening prayer each day and stiff penalties for slackers. The *Book of Common Prayer* contained morning and evening services and a complete Psalter, indicating which was to be prayed each day.[10] The Bible was read all the way through each year following the liturgical calendar. Among the Puritans, dissenters, Presbyterians, Huguenots, Quakers, and Congregationalists (and Baptists and Methodists after the onset of the Great Awakening of the 1740s), *sermons* far more than liturgy counted in worship. As can be seen from William Byrd II of Westover and James Blair (1685–1743), preaching loomed large. Byrd wrote that "Religion is the Duty which every Reasonable Creature owes to God, the Creator and Supream Governor of the World." This *duty* was best fulfilled through work, penance, and obedience, in a community where all were admittedly Christians. A merciful and good God had sent his Son into the world, they said, so as "to bring us to Heaven." Such faithful obedience is therapeutic for a human nature defaced by sin in fallen men, who originally had been created in God's image. Thus, men and women are exhorted to

9. Aristotle, *Politics* 3.11.4–5 1287a35, trans. H. Rackham, Loeb Classical Library (Cambridge, MA: Harvard University Press, 1977), 264–65. Trans. modified by author.

10. Bond, *Damned Souls*, 70; Handy, *History of the Churches*, 15.

imitate Christ by living holy lives: "Every man [that] doth not imitate God but [acts] contrary to him, is so far *unnatural* because he acts contrary to his natural pattern & exemplar." The human pilgrimage on earth thereby involves essentially the *restoration* of that ruined original nature as far that may be possible for each individual person with the help of divine Grace – as William Byrd taught and James Blair (the president of the College of William and Mary) concurred in one of his 117 discourses on the Sermon on the Mount, writings that filled five published volumes.[11] Man's pilgrimage to heaven was exemplified in John Bunyan's *Pilgrim's Progress* (1678) but had medieval roots.[12]

"Salutary neglect," as Edmund Burke termed it in the 1770s, was emphatically a way of life in Virginia from Jamestown onward, especially with the church chronically lacking clergy, supervision, money, and direction. Ordained ministers were scarce, making baptism difficult and celebration of the Lord's Supper infrequent. There was no American bishop until after the Revolution. Local customs both political and ecclesial tended to trump legislation and local practice to become law itself by common usage and prescription. An indigenous common law evolved in Virginia as it did elsewhere in America. In the absence of an episcopacy, the parish vestries independently engaged the ministers and otherwise governed the church. Composed of leading citizens (George Washington served as a vestryman) and thereby providing lay control by local elites, a new representative ecclesiastical order grew up. Vestries also tended to govern the counties within which they were located, thus forming (together with the county courts) the core institutions of the Virginia polity standing

---

11. Bond, *Damned Souls*, 250–51.
12. "The Anglican notion of the journey, however, possessed its own distinct qualities, emphasizing neither the terrors of the wilderness stage typical of Puritan writers nor the mystical union with God common among Roman Catholic authors. Likewise, they wrote little of the rapturous joy of sinners admitted to redemption. . . . Theirs was a low-key piety, deeply felt and involving the 'whole individual,' but given to order rather than to passion or ecstasy." Bond, *Damned Souls*, 245.

between the church authorities in London and the governor, council, and burgesses in Williamsburg as the key representative institution of governance.[13] "Local custom and local law both granted vestrymen authority to hire and fire clergy, and they had no intention of forfeiting rights they now [1683] counted among their property. A power used was a power assumed."[14]

II. Anthropology and ontology

Puritan New England and the other colonial experiences were highly variegated and may be contrasted, of course; but I must generalize, and for reasons already noticed kinship is palpable. John Winthrop in 1630, on board the *Arabella,* concluded his discourse entitled "A Model of Christian Charity" with the now-celebrated exhortation to the English Puritan settlers to keep their unity of the spirit and bond of peace of the community, diligently to live righteously and to seek holiness, so that "the Lord will be our God and delight to dwell among us, as his own people . . . [then] we shall find that the God of Israel is among us . . . for we must Consider that we shall be as a City upon a Hill, the eyes of all people are upon us. . . . Therefore let us choose life."[15] The Virginia plantation, in many respects, was another story. There the stress was on the commercial imperialism of England's Stuart kings, and the colony became valued for its profitable tobacco crops. As Sir Edward Seymour, one of Charles II's Lords of the Treasury, bluntly put it when the Virginians' religious plight came up and founding a college to alleviate it was proposed: "*Souls! Damn your Souls. Make Tobacco!*"[16]

13. Ibid., 196–214, 219.
14. Ibid., 218.
15. John Winthrop, "A Modell of Christian Charity," in *Political Thought in America: An Anthology,* 2nd ed., ed. Michael B. Levy (Long Grove, IL: Waveland Press, 1992), 12. Orthography modernized.
16. Quoted from Bond, *Damned Souls,* 194. The quotation is the book's epigraph. A recent general account of the Jamestown and early Virginia experiences can be found in Charles C. Mann, "America Found and Lost: Legacy of Jamestown," *National Geographic.Com/Magazine* (May 2007), 32–67. http://ngm.nationalgeographic.com/2007/05/jamestown/charles-mann-text.

But faith concerns persisted and were addressed. Decisive for religion in its biblical forms was the understanding of human nature and the meaning and scope of human existence within comprehensive reality. Admittedly God-centered, what did such a view of reality entail? Many things, to be sure, not least of all the familiar Creator- creaturely relationship generally affirmed in the Declaration of Independence in 1776 that indelibly vested each human being with inalienable attributes – among which were said to be rights to life, liberty, and the pursuit of Happiness. Standing behind that summarizing statement cast in neutral language is an anthropology and ontology derived from philosophy and revelation. Self-evident truths, these principles were susceptible to interpretation and ambiguous, as a consensual statement had to be; but they were never supplanted by the secularist revolution of Enlightenment rationalism ongoing in law and thought among some of the elites, as Washington took pains to remind everyone in his Farewell Address. Hence the Declaration was understood by a faithful community in broadly Christian rather than in primarily secular or narrowly sectarian terms, as John Adams said.

The decisive differentiation between classical Greek philosophical anthropology and the Christian theory of man turned, in effect, on the elaboration of Aristotle's conception of "immortalizing." He found this to be the fruit of the contemplative life that he thought best for man qua man and as the summit of happiness in the mature man, or *spoudaios*. Blessedness (*makarios*) is the more than merely mortal divine fruit of the virtuous life oriented toward Happiness (*eudaimonia*) as the highest good attainable by action. However, immortalizing becomes *holiness* in the biblical orbit of Christian revelation. It plainly lies beyond nature and the cosmos in the Beatitude of eternal salvation through faith in Christ and Union with God. The Greeks' *agnostos theos* (Acts 17:23) is revealed in Christ, Paul announces. The *summum bonum,* or highest Good (*Agathon*), discerned in the culmination of Plato's ascent, is experientially absorbed into God venerated as Creator and Savior, as companion and helper in the rise of divine fellowship. Erotic ascent to the Idea and the *philia* of Aristotle forming community, as well as the rise to participation in the immortalizing Good or divine, differentiates in Christian experience as the *agape* of the divine partner in being who loves us so that we may love him. This same divine love as Grace draws sinful man through conversion to rise from ruin (*amor sui* and *superbia vitae*) and move toward reconciliation (through *amor Dei*, in Augustine's terms). The person created in the divine image is once more restored through love to participate in the divine communion in faith and hope. There is nothing in Greek philosophy that attains the illumination of reality so gloriously as 1 John 4: "God is love. . . . We love him because he first loved us."[17] Finally it may be said that this ontological understanding of reality forms the heart of Thomas Aquinas's elaborate philosophy of man in terms of *amicitia* and *fides caritate formata,* the crowning achievement of medieval Scholastic philosophy. It is well to emphasize in a collectivizing age such as our own that primary human *reality* vests solely in singular human beings by this analysis, so that just as each human person uniquely possesses physical fingerprints or DNA, he also possesses ontological status and spiritual singularity as an *individual.*[18] To the point of immediate concerns, this understanding of human-divine reality structured existential *faith* as preached in English accents, during and after the powerful revival

17. 1 John 4:16, 19.
18. Cf. Thomas Aquinas, *Summa contra gentiles*, bk. 3: Providence, pt. 1, chap. 75, para. 13: "God is the cause of actual being. . . . Singulars are being, and more so than universals, for universals do not subsist of themselves, but are only in singulars. Therefore, divine providence applies to singulars" (trans. Vernon J. Bourke [New York: Doubleday, 1956], 253). In para. 15 of this chapter Thomas illustrates providential care by quoting Matt. 10:29 that even a sparrow "shall not fall to the ground without your Father" – the same verse invoked by Benjamin Franklin in the Federal Convention when reminding delegates of divine concern for human affairs and the need for help from our "Friend": "*God governs in the affairs of men.* And if a sparrow cannot fall to the ground without his notice, is it probable than an empire can rise without his aid?" Franklin's speech of June 28, 1787, quoted and referenced in Sandoz, *A Government of Laws,* 161.

movement in eighteenth-century America we call the Great Awakening, by such luminaries as John Wesley, George Whitefield, Gilbert and William Tennent, and Jonathan Edwards.[19] John Wesley corrected the old philosophers' anthropology by finding that *reason* – and most particularly not the truncated "reason" of those atheist-pests, the Enlightened *philosophes* – is not the *differentia specifica* of man. Rather, the real distinguishing difference of man is his uniquely human capacity for communion with the divine: Only the human being is capable of God.

III. Constitutional implications

Such a lofty conception of human existence and of the human person obviously burst the bounds of political systems and must find representation beyond politics in the church – essentially an Augustinian insight and solution that superseded the classic philosopher's search for the paradigmatic polity and, in various degrees of success, forestalled the expansive perfectionism of millenarians, chiliasts, and the various modern gnostic and other immanentizing zealots into the present. While partaking of the optimism of especially the British Enlightenment through John Locke and common sense philosophy, the core of the moderation expected of human enterprise was preserved in the American founding: There were no utopians in the Federal Convention of 1787, we are told. Men are not angels and, short of the General Resurrection, are unlikely ever to become such in this world. Meanwhile the Creation and its goodness is to be enjoyed, life is to be lived, and a dangerous world kept at bay. The spiritual culture and philosophical sophistication I have limned has inoculated America against most of the worst pitfalls of ideological politics – at least so far! (Fingers crossed.) The anthropology and prevailing ethos of the late eighteenth century bore direct fruit in the

---

19. For details see Ellis Sandoz, *Republicanism, Religion, and the Soul of America* (Columbia: University of Missouri Press, 2006), esp. chap. 1.

formation of the Union. We still have a republic, if we can keep it.

Conclusion: *A True Map of Man*[20]

While the American Founders relied on Aristotle and Cicero and cited Montesquieu, they understood with Saint Paul that "all have sinned, and come short of the glory of God" (Rom 3:23; cf. 1 Tim. 1:15). They, therefore, accepted the corollary drawn by the judicious Hooker that laws can rightly be made only by assuming that men are so depraved as to be hardly better than wild beasts[21] –

20. This section incorporates ibid., chap. 1, §8, pp. 47–51, with minor changes.
21. Cf. *Federalist No. 6*. Thus, Richard Hooker, *Of the Laws of Ecclesiastical Polity* [1593], ed. A. S. McGrade, Cambridge Texts in the History of Political Thought (Cambridge: Cambridge University Press, 1989), in bk. 1.10.1, writes: "Laws politic, ordained for external order and regiment amongst men, are never framed as they should be, unless presuming the will of man to be inwardly obstinate, rebellious, and averse from all obedience unto the sacred laws of his nature; in a word, unless presuming man to be in regard of his depraved mind little better than a wild beast, they do accordingly provide notwithstanding so to frame his outward actions, that they be no hindrance unto the common good for which societies are instituted: unless they do this, they are not perfect" (ibid., 87–88). Similarly Machiavelli: "All writers on politics have pointed out . . . that in constituting and legislating for a commonwealth it must needs be taken for granted that all men are wicked and that they will always give vent to malignity that is in their minds when opportunity offers." *The Discourses* 1.3, ed. Bernard Crick (Harmondsworth: Penguin Books, 1974), 112. Indeed, the tension between the reason of the law and the passion of the human being is fundamental to the philosophical anthropology underlying the whole conception of rule of law and of a government of laws and not of men, from Aristotle onward. Cf. the *locus classicus*: "He who asks law (*nomos*) to rule is asking God and intelligence (reason, *nous*) alone to rule; while he who asks for the rule of a human being is importing a wild beast too; for desire is like a wild beast, and anger perverts rulers and the very best of men. Hence the law is intelligence without appetition." Aristotle, *Politics* 3.16, 1287a23–31, trans. T. A. Sinclair, rev. Trevor J. Saunders (Harmondsworth: Penguin Books, 1891), 226. Quoted in the text *supra*, at n9. In sum, as stated elsewhere: "In fact, my axiom of politics (a minor contribution to the science) is this: *Human beings are virtually ungovernable*. After all, human beings in addition to possessing reason and gifts of conscience are material, corporeal,

even though they are created a little lower than the angels and beloved of God their Creator (Ps. 8).

To generalize and simplify, but not to argue perfect homogeneity: From the Anglo-Norman Anonymous and John Wycliffe to John Wesley, John Adams, and Abraham Lincoln's invocation of "government of the people, by the people, and for the people," lines of religious development undergirded and fostered a shared sense of the sanctity of the individual human being living in immediacy to God and associated the Christian calling to imitate God in their lives with political duty, capacity for self-government, *salus populi,* and the ethic of aspiration through love of God. From this fertile ground emerged the institutions of civil society and republicanism perfected in the American founding.

Among other things, the Framers – faced with the weighty challenge of how to make free government work – banked the fires of zealotry and political millenarianism in favor of latitudinarian faith and a quasi-Augustinian understanding of the two cities. They humbly bowed before the inscrutable mystery of history and the human condition with its suffering and imperfection and accepted watchful waiting for fulfillment of a Providential destiny known only to God – whose "kingdom is not of this world" (John 18:36). But in addition to understanding government as a necessary coercive restraint on the sinful creature, as we have seen, they reflected a faith that political practice in perfecting the image of God in every man through just dominion was *itself* a blessed vocation and the calling of free men: It was stewardship in imitation of God's care for His freely created and sustained world, one enabled solely by the grace bestowed on individuals and a favored community. They embraced freedom of conscience as quintessential liberty for a citizenry of free men and women, as had John Milton long before who exclaimed in *Areopagitica:* "Give me the liberty to know, to utter, and to argue

passionate, self-serving, devious, obstreperous, ornery, unreliable, imperfect, fallible, and prone to sin if not outright depraved. And we have some bad qualities besides." Sandoz, *The Politics of Truth*, 39.

freely according to conscience, above all liberties." And, for better or worse, they followed Milton (as well as Roger Williams and John Locke) in heeding his plea "to leave the church to itself" and "not suffer the two powers, the ecclesiastical and the civil, which are so totally distinct, to commit whoredom together."[22] The correlate was religious toleration within limits, as necessary for the existence of a flourishing *civil society* whose free operations minimized tampering with religious institutions or dogmas. Yet the historically affirmed vocation of a special people under God still could be pursued through active devotion to public good, liberty, and justice solidly grounded in Judaeo-Christian transcendentalism. Citizens were at the same time self-consciously also pilgrims, aware that this world is not their home. It is this ever-present living tension with the divine Ground above all else, perhaps, that has made the United States so nearly immune politically to the ideological maladies that have characterized much of the modern world, such as fascism and Marxism and, lately, fanatical jihadism.

Like all of politics, the Founders' solutions were compromises, offensive to utopians and all other flaming idealists. But this may be no detraction from their work, since despite all national vicissitudes, we still today strive to keep our republic – under the world's oldest existing Constitution. Moreover, there has yet to appear an American dictator, after 230 years of national existence; and the United States, at grievous cost in lives and treasure, has

---

22. Milton, *Areopagitica and Other Political Writings*, ed. John Alvis (Indianapolis: Liberty Fund, 1999), 44 and 406. Cf. John Locke, *Writings on Religion*, ed. Victor Nuovo (Oxford: Oxford University Press, 2002), 73–82; also Edwin S. Gaustad, *Liberty of Conscience: Roger Williams in America* (Grand Rapids, MI: Eerdmans Publishing, 1991), who writes at 219: "In the past half-century, American society has become noisily and notoriously pluralistic. This has made Roger Williams more relevant, for he had strong opinions about what government should do about religious pluralism: leave it alone. Turks, Jews, infidels, papists: leave them alone. . . . Religion has the power to persuade, never the power to compel. Government does have the power to compel, but that government is wisest and best which offers to liberty of conscience its widest possible range."

steadily stood in wars of global reach as the champion of freedom in the face of raging despotisms of every description.

To conclude then: Let us not overlook the secret that a sound map of human nature lies at the heart of the Constitution of the United States and its institutional arrangements. Men are not angels, and government, admittedly, is the greatest of all reflections on human nature: The *demos* ever tends to become the *ochlos* – even if there could be a population of philosophers and saints – and constantly threatens majoritarian tyranny. Merely mortal magistrates, no less than self-serving factions, riven by *superbia*, avarice, and *libido dominandi*, must be restrained artfully by a vast net of adversarial devices if just government is to have any chance of prevailing over human passions while still nurturing the liberty of free men. To attain these noble ends in what is called a government of laws and not of men, it was daringly thought, perhaps ambition could effectively counteract ambition and, as one more *felix culpa*, therewith supply the defect of better motives. This is most dramatically achieved through the routine operations of the central mechanisms of divided and separated powers and of checks and balances that display the genius of the Constitution and serve as the hallmark of America's republican experiment itself. *All of this would have been quite inconceivable without a Christian anthropology, enriched by classical political theory and the common-law tradition, as uniquely embedded in the* habits of the American people at the time of the Founding and nurtured thereafter. On this ground an extended commercial republic flourished and America became a light to the nations.[23]

Nagging questions remain: Can a political order ultimately grounded in the tension toward transcendent divine Being, memorably proclaimed in the Declaration of Independence and solidly informed by biblical revelation and philosophy, indefinitely endure – resilient though it may be – in the face of nihilistic assault on this vital spiritual tension by every means, including by the

---

23. The text here follows Sandoz, *Republicanism, Religion, and the Soul of America*, 49–52.

very institutions of liberty themselves? Perhaps these are only growing pains that afflict us, rather than the disintegration of our civilization. The positivist, scientistic, and Marxist climate of opinion is so pervasive and intellectually debilitating in the public arena and universities that it often turns philosophical and religious discourse into incomprehensible oddities whose meaning is lost to consciousness amid the din of deformation and deculturation. For instance, the "walls of separation between these two [church and state] must forever be upheld," Richard Hooker wrote in contemptuously characterizing religious zealots of his distant time. By way of Thomas Jefferson's famous 1801 letter and the U.S. Supreme Court more recently, that metaphor now lives on as the shibboleth of strange new fanatics of our own day, including those sometimes identified as atheist humanists.[24] Thus, even as religious revival today enlivens American spirituality, we still endure the strong cross-currents of intellectual, moral, and social disarray of the republic – and not of the American republic alone. We test our faith that the truth shall prevail and look for hopeful signs on the horizon. We also remember that both revealed truth and philosophical reason ever have been nurtured by resolute individuals' resistance to social corruption and apostasy, in what may perchance once again become some saving remnant.

IV. Postscript on freedom of conscience

Finally, a comment on the vexed problem of toleration or *freedom of conscience,* as Thomas Jefferson and James Madison insisted we call it. Possessors of absolute Truth, especially when it is taken to be salvific, do not readily extend benevolence to the benighted folk who reject or disdain it. Killing in righteous wrath is far more likely, not to say enjoyable, in such a noble cause. Just ask Bloody Mary's allies, or Cromwell's army in Ireland, or survivors of Saint

24. Hooker, *Laws of Ecclesiastical Polity,* bk. 8.1.2, p. 131; Everson v. United States, 330 U.S. 1 (1947) at 15–16; cf. the classic study by Henri de Lubac, *The Drama of Atheist Humanism,* trans. E. M. Riley (London: Sheed & Ward, 1949).

Bartholomew, or descendants of the 800,000 Huguenots who finally fled France after revocation of the Edict of Nantes in 1685, or read about the radical jihadists in this morning's newspaper. This carnage, all committed in the name of *Truth*, is piddling in comparison with the Holocaust and the Gulag and similar events of the ideological and enlightened age in which we live, of course – and the point is to be stressed: One scholar has tabulated the victims of the contemporary dogmatomachy (excluding war dead) since 1900 at nearly 120 million murdered at their own governments' hands, more than 95 million of them killed by Marxist regimes.[25]

Democracy is said to be the worst form of government – except for all the others. Something similar might be said of toleration, and zealots in our midst ought to take the lesson to heart. Fanaticism yet lives, as we observe. The great French spiritualist, philosopher, and judge Jean Bodin (d. 1596, barely escaping death from the Catholic League) gave a great soul's solution to persecution and religious warfare by concluding that "true religion is nothing but the turning [*conversio*] of a purified mind toward the true God."[26] Lamenting that "diabolical Hell-conceived principle of persecution" raging in the Virginia of his youth, James Madison himself seems to have shared just this sentiment. It propelled him into politics as the foundation of his own prudential science and life as statesman. Its first legislative fruit was revision of George Mason's draft of the Virginia Declaration of Rights of 1776 to make it read: "16. That Religion, or the duty which we owe to our Creator, and the manner of discharging it, can be directed only by reason and conviction, not by force or violence."[27] Madison's masterly case for religious liberty given in the

25. R. J. Rummel, *Lethal Politics: Soviet Politics and Mass Murder* (New Brunswick, NJ: Transaction Pubs., 1990), ix.

26. Jean Bodin, "Letter to Jean Bautru," quoted from Eric Voegelin, *History of Political Ideas*, vol. 5, *Religion and the Rise of Modernity*, ed. James L. Wiser (Columbia: University of Missouri Press, 1998), 188, vol. 23 of *The Collected Works of Eric Voegelin*, 34 vols.

27. Bernard Schwartz, *The Bill of Rights: A Documentary History*, 2 vols. (New York: Chelsea House, 1971), 1:236, quoting Virginia Declaration of Rights of 1776.

"Memorial and Remonstrance Against Religious Assessments" followed in 1785, and its adoption effectively blocked reestablishment of the Episcopal Church in Virginia. This, in turn, paved the way for enactment six months later (while he was in Paris) of Jefferson's long dormant "Statute for Religious Freedom," which premises that "Almighty God hath created the mind free." A scholar writes: "The troops were Baptists and Presbyterians and the tactics were Madison's, but the words . . . were Jefferson's."[28] Then in the First Congress under the Constitution came Madison's leadership in fashioning the Federal Bill of Rights, including the First Amendment, which opens with the religion clauses: "Congress shall make no law respecting an establishment of religion, or prohibiting the free exercise thereof."[29] When compared with the "torrents of blood" Madison from history and observation knew to be the likely alternative, these pragmatic protections of freedom of conscience doubtless compose one of the supreme achievements of American statesmanship.

28. Henry F. May as quoted, along with the preceding material in this paragraph, drawn from Sandoz, "Religious Liberty and Religion in the American Founding," in *The Politics of Truth*, chap. 5, p. 80.
29. See the account in Sandoz, *Government of Laws*, 203–8, 215–17.

3. So What's the Difference? The Debate over American Independence

In a particularly frenzied debate over *Equality* in the Constituent Assembly during the French Revolution, the old story goes, one citizen-deputy enthusiastically affirmed that "there is very little difference between men and women!" At which assertion the entire body rose to its feet shouting, "*Vive la différence!*"

So it was with Britain and America during the period of the Founding, although the little difference might not have been quite so entertaining. Still, everything important seemed to be quite the same: language, religion, ethnicity, political institutions and practices, legal heritage, patrimony, allegiances. Paradoxically, everything was the same and yet totally different, depending on perspective and interpretation.

Viewed from the end of the process, the little difference is magnified. The United States emerged from it a republic (if we can keep it) and Great Britain remained a monarchy and empire, even without most of its North American colonies. From the Stamp Act (1765) through the Battle of New Orleans (1815), what began as discussion became debate, and debate became war not once but twice. To their chagrin and astonishment, the Brits lost both times – convincingly at Yorktown with French help, decisively in the Chalmette swamp, where the crack Black Watch (93rd Highlanders) and several elite units fresh from sacking and burning Baltimore and Washington were decimated by Barataria pirates and Tennessee frontiersmen commanded by Jean Lafitte and Andrew Jackson. The Chalmette encounter ended with 2,600 British killed compared to 8 American dead and 13 wounded. The common man took his rise. In the passionate course of these events America defined itself, by a process that continued – and may even be said to continue into the present.

The incipient characteristics and principles distinguishing America and the American mind emerged during what began as a civil war – the worst kind of warfare, as we know. Ezra Stiles, the Congregational minister and president of Yale during the Revolution, was convinced that the Scots (led by John Witherspoon and James Wilson) were instrumental and that America might have patched things up with the mother country but for their fomenting discontent and rebellion.[1] Salient attributes of difference between the two countries became evident.

1. First, there was a kind of dogged literal-minded insistence born of pervasive Evangelical Christianity and a legalist cast of mind that words mean what they say, especially such words as *consent* and *representation*. "Laws they are not which public approbation hath not made so," the judicious Hooker had elegantly intoned, John Locke repeated, and Americans believed. This meant *real* consent by *real* representatives – not some fanciful virtual representation in a remote Parliament having no electoral connection with American constituents and notoriously corrupted by Robinarchy. This is the bedrock of free government for free men, and nothing less would suffice. Samuel Adams was especially clear on the matter. In 1765, Adams wrote to the governor on behalf of the Massachusetts House of Representatives:

> Zealous advocates for the constitution usually compared their acts of Parliament with Magna Charta; and if it ever happened that such acts were made as infringed upon the rights of that charter, they were always repealed. . . . There

---

1. Cf. Ezra Stiles, *The Literary Diary of Ezra Stiles*, ed. Franklin B. Dexter, 3 vols. (New York: Charles Scribners' Sons, 1901), 2:184–85: "There are only two Scotchmen in Congress, viz. Dr. Witherspoon . . . & Mr. Wilson. . . . Both strongly national, & can't bear any Thing in Congress which reflects on Scotland. . . . Let us boldly say, for History will say it, that the whole of this War is so far chargeable to the Scotch Councils, & to the Scotch as a Nation (for they have nationally come into it) as that had it not been for them, this Quarrel had never happened." Dated July 23, 1777.

are certain *original inherent rights* belonging to the people, which the Parliament itself cannot divest them of, consistent with their own constitution: among these is the right of representation in the same body which exercises the power of taxation. . . . The right of the colonies to make their own laws and tax themselves has never been questioned. . . . The very supposition that the Parliament, through the supreme power over the subjects of Britain universally, should yet conceive of a despotic power within themselves, would be most disrespectful. . . . To suppose an indisputable right in any government, to tax the subjects without their consent, [includes] the idea of such a power.[2]

John Witherspoon, James Madison's mentor at Princeton, remarked that "the generous principles of universal liberty" are incomprehensible to the British, who think Parliament can do anything and who, therefore, "consider the liberty of their country itself as consisting in the dominion of the House of Commons."[3]

2. The *liber homo – free man –* of Magna Carta was alive and well and living in Boston, Philadelphia, and Charleston.[4] With a painful firsthand knowledge of slavery, Americans knew it when they saw it, and the Declaratory Act (1766) undoubtedly was it. Edmund Burke (as well as Pitt and Camden) knew it too and scathingly denounced the ministry to within an inch of committing treason on the floor of the House of Commons for abandoning the great heritage of English freedom and embracing slavery

2. "Answer of the House of Representatives of Massachusetts to the Governor's Speech. October 23, 1765," in *The Writings of Samuel Adams*, ed. Harry A. Cushing, 4 vols. (New York: Octagon Books, 1968), 1:13–18. Capitalization modified and italics added.

3. Quoted from Ellis Sandoz, *A Government of Laws: Political Theory, Religion, and the American Founding* (1990; repr. Columbia: University of Missouri Press, 2001), 165.

4. For the term *liber homo* in the 1225 Magna Carta, which became the first statute of the realm in 1297, see esp. chaps. 1, 14, 24, 29, and 32. On the meaning of the term, see the discussion of J. C. Holt, *Magna Carta*, 2nd ed. (1964; repr. Cambridge: Cambridge University Press, 1992), esp.10–20, 276–80: "It was a grant to all free men throughout the realm" (276).

for the Englishmen in America, as a weed that grows in every soil, thereby stabbing their very vitals. Moreover, Burke observed, if you can do it to Englishmen with your army there you can do it as well to countrymen who stayed at home. In his old age a half-century later, the last of the Founders, James Madison, still found the argument cogent and esteemed his countrymen for their perspicacity in seeing the hand of *tyranny* in a three-penny tax on tea.

3. Liberty and tyranny were the antipodes of the political and constitutional argument. The categories were as old as Aristotle, Cicero, and the immemorial English constitution, as ancient as coercive Nimrod and the free republic of Elders in Israel. Religion and metaphysics as well as mere political theory were in play and gave great resonance to related assertions – as the Declaration of Independence itself succinctly stated the familiar case. A cool rationalism such as Jefferson's might have declared the independence of such folk but could never have persuaded them to fight for it, Perry Miller observed. And he added that the Revolution itself was preached as a revival and had the astonishing result of succeeding, a conclusion borne out by recent scholarship. Patriotism without piety is mere grimace, one Philadelphia preacher thundered. "The Sabbath was made for man, not man for the Sabbath" (Mark 2:27) – and the same held true of government. "We are not children of the bondwoman, but of the free" (Gal. 4:31) became an unlikely rallying cry, as did also: "We ought to obey God rather than men" (Acts 5:29) and "If God be for us, who can be against us?" (Rom. 8:31). Celebrated elements of the American political theology therewith appeared and were propagated by James Otis's "black regiment," but not only his. We remember the practice of James Madison (cousin of the president, later Bishop Madison, president of the College of William and Mary who led his students into battle) who sometimes prayed the Lord's Prayer with the words, "thy *Republic* come, Thy will be done on earth as it is in heaven."

4. Then, there was natural law with correlative natural rights as abiding structures that drew from the biblical, classical, and medieval horizons of faith and from Enlightenment philosophy in

an eclectic fashion. However noble and enduring the English constitution and its celebrated liberties, the transcendent reality of God and hegemonic nature loomed supreme and beyond all human devising in *recta ratio* as the providential sources of order and justice. But this generous understanding already was reflected in Gratian and affirmed by Thomas Aquinas: "The natural law is what is contained in the Law and the Gospel . . . by which everyone is commanded to do to others as he would be done by": All law is founded on the Golden Rule, in other words (Matt.7:12). "An unjust law is no law at all," Augustine wrote, Aquinas repeated,[5] and Martin Luther King made the centerpiece of the civil rights revolution. Liberty itself had been instilled into human nature by the hand of God, Sir John Fortescue affirmed, in what has been called the Englishing of Thomism in the fifteenth century. Sir Edward Coke agreed, as did Jefferson and the Adamses, in 1776. This settled conviction supplied the groundwork for *inalienable* rights in men who had been created equal by their Creator and, consequently, might rightly aspire to *political* equality as well – the common sense of the subject, Jefferson later called it, and an augury of the democratic republicanism to come. At the concrete level of the American debate, Camden declared that "taxation and representation are inseparably united: This position is founded on the laws of *nature: It is more: It is itself an eternal law of nature* – Whatever is a man's own is absolutely his own; and no man has a right to take it from him without his consent. . . . Whoever does it, commits a Robbery: *He throws down the distinction between liberty and slavery.*"[6]

5. Constitutionally, the Framers in 1787 placed their "true map of man" (as John Adams called their philosophical anthropology) at the center of the self-equilibrating institutional order as

---

5. *De lib. Arb.* 1.5 in *Summa theologica* I–II, q.96: "The like are acts of violence rather than laws, because, as Augustine says, 'A law that is not just, seems to be no law at all.'" Dino Bigongiari, ed. and intro., *The Political Ideas of St. Thomas Aquinas: Representative Selections* (New York: Hafner, 1969), 72.
6. Quoted by Samuel Adams, *Writings*, 2:302.

the chief technical means of achieving a government of laws and not of men, conceived as a noble residue of the operation of separated and divided powers textured by an intricate web of adversarial checking. This ingeniously helped supply for fallible and self-serving men the defects of better motives, Madison said. It did so, also, without sacrificing the possibility in the Supreme Law of the Land of an energetic Executive when that might be called for; even Plato insisted that his philosopher-king (who might be a woman, we remember) had to be a person best in both philosophy and in *war,* given the human condition (*Republic* 543–44). The novel Philadelphia vision of a compound mixed republic was persuasively explained in *The Federalist* – with palpable echoes back to Aristotle, Cicero, Aquinas (the first Whig, Acton thought), Charles I's 1642 *Answer to the Nineteen Propositions of Parliament,* and the Cromwellian commonwealth or *republic.* This had lasted a mere twelve years, ended with the Restoration, and was said to have been buried in an unmarked grave after the English Glorious Revolution and Settlement of 1689 – only to be resurrected in splendor in America a century later.

What had been *wrong* in the eighteenth century was not the British constitution itself, as venerated by everyone from Montesquieu to John Adams, but the abandonment of Old Whig principles in favor of imperial hubris and *libido dominandi.* This error was amply reflected in policy grown insufferable in American eyes but also in theory as propounded by the "honeyed Mansfieldism" of Blackstone with its embrace of the principle of an irresistible "supreme power" vested in Parliament along with the undergirding natural-right theories of Grotius and Puffendorf making these "absolute" in autonomous human beings – who might thereby absolutely reject as well as claim them. Hobbes is reborn, and the positivist jurisprudence of John Austin looms. The recourse to transcendence was thus cast aside. The effect of a naturalistic reduction of this magnitude was to sever the anchoring in divine Being, invoked in the Declaration of Independence and insisted on by a faithful community that resolutely interpreted politics and history in biblical and Providential terms. The result was philosophically unacceptable and became politically repugnant when unmasked as a smokescreen concealing old-fashioned tyranny. So it seemed, in any event. In the spirit of the Pelican chorus, I think so then and thought so still.

Thus, the American adaptations of their precious English and broadly Western heritage aimed at justice and insisted on personal and corporate liberty, not simply at independence at any cost as some then suspected. The Constitution required a Bill of Rights for ratification. It also required guardians of those rights against majoritarian tyranny in an independent judiciary. The power of judicial review established in *Marbury v. Madison* (1803) was anticipated by Coke in *Dr. Bonham's Case* (1610) but was, of course, rejected by Blackstone. "Parliament can do anything but make a man a woman and a woman a man," Lord Herbert hopefully remarked in the seventeenth century – a minor impediment lately removed by Danish medicine. Albert Dicey, effectively confirming the obnoxious claim of the old Declaratory Act more than a century later, nailed the door shut in 1885 by summarizing how things stood: "Parliament . . . has . . . the right to make or unmake any law whatever; . . . no person or body is recognised by the law of England as having a right to override or set aside the legislation of Parliament."[7] The Founders knew what they were doing, after all. There had been no misunderstanding.

Sovereignty shifted to popular or constituent sovereignty in America, where it was said "the People are king," a matter vexed by "this mixed Constitution" composed of sovereign states.[8] Parliamentary sovereignty and ministerial responsibility formed the British path. The American adaptations manifested continuity but took quite a different and less decisive path, favoring an empire of Liberty under law. The Founders relied on an admirable store of *experience* in self-government and public affairs, the fruit of long "salutary neglect" to be sure, but also of admirable

---

7. A. V. Dicey, *Introduction to the Study of the Law of the Constitution*, 8th ed. (1915; repr. Indianapolis: Liberty Classics, n.d.), 3–4.
8. Cf. *The Federalist, Nos. 39* and *40*. Quoted phrase is on p. 247 in the Rossiter edition (New York: New American Library, 1961).

sophistication and astute practice in self-government and constitution-making.

The statesmen of the period, thus, drew upon the prudential science of the old Greeks, such as that esteemed in Aristotle's *phronimos* and in Tully; upon the enlightened faith of a citizenry long practiced in the operations of free institutions – economic, political, and ecclesiastical; and upon what they themselves called "the divine science of politics." Their noble synthesis made all the difference for republican free government on the presidential model, then and now. Finally, they also lay claim under divine Providence to the high ground of history, expressing the prayerful hope "that the rod of tyrants may be broken into pieces, and the oppressed be made Free – That wars may cease in all the Earth, and that confusions that are and have been among the Nations may be overruled" so that Peace might prevail.[9]

Vive la différence!

---

9.   "A Proclamation for a Day of Solemn Fasting and Prayer," March 20, 1797, in *Writings of Samuel Adams,* 4:407. The proclamation's text quoted continues: "for the promoting and speedily bringing on that holy and happy period, when the Kingdom of our Lord and Saviour Jesus Christ may be everywhere established, and all the people willingly bow to the Sceptre of Him who is the Prince of Peace" (ibid.).

4. The United States in the World Arena

The 9/11 Era and President Bush II

The question is: What is the proper role of the United States in contemporary world affairs? My answer is that it must be what it has always been: To serve liberty and justice as best we can while defending our security and national interests. None of these terms is susceptible of tidy definition, of course. And the world has changed significantly if not fundamentally since I first put these thoughts on paper. Not least of all, the Bush Administration has been succeeded by the Obama Administration. Still, basics remain arguably the same, and Islamist terrorism is a major focus.

1. Foreign Policy

No entangling alliances, despite abiding appeal to isolationists, xenophobes, and pacifists, didn't take us very far. It was effectively repudiated with the Louisiana Purchase, which paved the way for Manifest Destiny. After the lessons taught by the War of 1812, the Monroe Doctrine in 1823 asserted the enduring principles that the United States is to be *active* in the world arena and that it stood against colonialism or lesser use of force within its sphere of influence, then understood primarily as North and South America – but not forgetting the Barbary pirates and their ilk. This drawing of a line in the sand and daring anybody to cross it without suffering consequences has characterized U.S. foreign policy since that time. Speak softly and carry a big stick became explicit in the Roosevelt corollary. With the collapse of British power, the interest sphere expanded to encompass the rest of the free world during the Cold War, only so long as vital American interests are implicated. This included communist expansion or potential expansion (the Truman doctrine later elaborated by Walt Rostow) or any threat to vital national security interests judged sufficient to warrant diplomatic or military action. "Containment" positively meant keeping the world safe for democracy and out of the hands of totalitarian and especially communist despots – as first demonstrated on a large scale in the Korean conflict, where major United States military assets were deployed with beneficial lasting results from 1950 until today.

2. Bush II Administration Doctrine

From the time of the Founding there has been a moralistic if not plainly religious tinge to these policies, grounded like the country itself on the "laws of Nature and nature's God" as "self-evident truths" and felt to be an "almost chosen people" blessed by Providence, a light unto the nations. America did not have to wait for Woodrow Wilson to become righteous. It understood and represented itself as a force for good against palpable evil and tyranny from its beginning – not to mention Abraham Lincoln or *The Battle Hymn of the Republic*. Thus it was also in the wars of the twentieth century, whose rich rhetoric is familiar to all of us – with varying degrees of public acceptance of this overriding justification for action from the high ground while still attending to mundane military, economic, and geopolitical threats. A moral justification in addition to calculated rationality and interests has been judged essential in this country, if public support is to be marshaled and sustained for any period of time. The failure or inability for various reasons to do so (a potent Left and biased media among others) ultimately doomed the Vietnam policy of Kennedy and Johnson.

3. Post 9/11

The trauma of this malicious Islamist attack engendered a shift in policy emphasis, from sturdy deterrence and old Cold War containment to proactive diplomatic and military initiative. *Preemption* as a dimension of Just War theory, and of the universal right to self-defense, was not new with the Bush administration (e.g., Bay of Pigs, Grenada), nor does it signal imperialistic designs, much less eschatological intoxication – as the loud Left and our more excitable citizens sometimes clamorously assert. But it takes on sober importance (to include preventive war) as an option of last resort in an era of lethal danger from weapons of mass destruction, when absorbing the first punch could involve unacceptable risk or a possible knockout. As Secretary of State Condoleeza Rice said in 2002, "The risks of waiting must far outweigh the risks of action."

Not completely new – think of post–Civil War Reconstruction, the Open Door to China, and the Marshall Plan, for instance – but more novel and ambitious is the express and energetic pursuit of *transformative* policies. These are calculated to foster by all available means the move of nations to liberal market economies and democratic free governments worldwide as the *primary* prophylaxis against hostility and deadly threat from regimes or from the fanatical enclaves they may finance or harbor.[1]

4. Core Current Policy

This is different in tone and perhaps of more dubious validity. It rests on the convictions (as formulated on March 16, 2006) that

> the survival of liberty in our land increasingly depends on the success of liberty in other lands. The best hope for peace in our world is the expansion of freedom in all the world. . . . To protect our Nation and honor our values, the United States seeks to extend freedom across the globe by leading an international effort to end tyranny and to promote effective democracy. We will employ the full array of political, economic, diplomatic, and other tools at our disposal [to that end]. . . . We have a responsibility to promote human freedom. Yet freedom cannot be imposed; it must be chosen. The form that freedom and democracy take in any land will reflect the history, culture,

1. Cf. the account in George W. Bush, *Decision Points* (New York: Crown Publishers, 2010), chap. 13, "Freedom Agenda," 395–438.

and habits unique to its people. . . . The advance of freedom and human dignity through democracy is the long-term solution to the transnational terrorism of today. . . . There are four steps we will take in the short term: We will 1) prevent attacks by terrorist networks before they occur; 2) deny WMD to rogue states and to terrorist allies who would use them without hesitation; 3) deny terrorist groups the support and sanctuary of rogue states; and 4) deny the terrorists control of any nation that they would use as a base and launching pad for terror.[2]

5. Pragmatism and Politics

As previously noticed, Davy Crockett's motto was "Figure out what's right and go ahead!"[3] This maxim well expresses the spirit of the George W. Bush foreign policy in the war on terrorism: It is simple, honest, and moralistic. It is pure Texas (and Methodist) Sunday school, one might even say – and we have to take President Bush's religious convictions seriously because he takes them seriously himself. It leads with the American trump card by transforming American *exceptionalism* into a universal movement: one invoking a universal human nature and identifying individual liberty as natural to all human beings – a defining God-given attribute and inalienable right. It also favors free market global economics and fosters an international community of sovereign free democratic states. On the key point President Bush remarked at a press conference on April 13, 2004: "I have this belief, strong belief, that freedom is not this country's gift to the world. Freedom is the Almighty's gift to every man and woman in this world."

Can such policy also be *realistic*? Is it a shimmering, even intoxicating, fantasy incapable of realization in the world at large,

---

2. Quoted from "The President's National Security Strategy," March 16, 2006, released by the White House.
3. Quoted from http://www.goodreads.com/author/quotes/147674.David_Crockett.

one doomed to exacerbate international conflict rather than ameliorate it? Perhaps so, sad to say. Perhaps as realistic as drawing to an inside straight, if you play poker. However: Better a bold policy than a timid one, or no policy at all, in an ineluctable high-stakes game where losing is no option. Besides: God takes care of children, drunks, and the United States of America, we cheerfully remember.

6. Potholes in the Road to Peace

Nobody said this would be easy, and criticism abounds. For instance:

* Woodrow Wilson couldn't do it and neither can George W. Bush. But the United States was not then the preeminent world leader, hegemonic or superpower, and economy.

* The whole endeavor has a destabilizing effect on global politics: Safe and friendly authoritarian regimes are better than hostile pseudo-democratic ones in the hands of terrorist entities like Hamas. This is madness we hear. (Bring Saddam back?)

* The other nations of the world will never accede to such blatant Westernization/Americanization and/or secularization. Even (especially?) Europe is skeptical. It is either too religious or too secular. Maybe. The American public – hearing the incessant clamor of the hollow men composing the world's ideologized self-anointed "elites" – has no stomach for the kind of dissensus or for the protracted conflict and carnage before us. Isolation and pacifism are too strong in America to sustain the effort essential to even modest success. Anyway, we don't like imperialism, so bring the boys and girls home and set up a perimeter around San Francisco, our last bastion of resolute true-blue patriotism.

* In the media age of information overload, deculturation, manipulation of public opinion, and vitriolic politics, blood on the TV screens 24/7 dramatizing the horrors of war

makes the whole effort patently un-American, not to mention plain distasteful. Too many casualties! Where's the good news? The price is too high! And for what?

* We'll go broke in the process. Iraq may now be costing roughly a billion dollars per week, we're told; the deficit is soaring, the national debt threatens the economic foundations of the Republic: We can't afford the war on terrorism. Embrace peace in our time. The Soviets couldn't afford the Cold War; how can we afford this one? By making the tax cuts permanent?

* Rampant *anti-Americanism* has exploded both at home and abroad because of Bush policy. We've lost all our friends, and politics has seldom been more polarized. Nobody remembers or cares that we saved the world from Adolf Hitler, from Tojo Hideki, and, later, from the Sino-Soviet evil empire in Central Europe and in Korea. Class-struggle fanatics, having mastered only one flawed text, monotonously decry a dark geopolitical capitalist plot. Peaceniks incapable of constructive action occupy Wall Street and burn our flag in indignation that we seek to foster regimes devoted to honesty, justice, and individual liberty. Pass the soma. Give us the peace of secure serfdom is the cry! – like those oppressed by Dostoevsky's Grand Inquisitor for whom hated freedom was the ultimate tyranny, personal responsibility. Away with all your principles! We want to be loved!

7. Reality Check

* The world has gone from 20 to some 120 democratic nations since the Second World War. If there is a wave of the future in global affairs, this is plainly it.

* If Indonesia and Turkey can democratize ("rowdy" or not), there is some reasonable hope for the rest of the Islamic world, even if not in accordance with Western models of free governments – a fact explicitly recognized by Bush

policy. Don't expect uniform results, but do look for amelioration of traditional systems. Politics is the art of the possible, some sage once said. Economic freedom may induce political freedom. Watch China and find out. It's worth a try in any case, since it brings better lives to all men and women – as can be seen everywhere it exists.

* Battle casualties are a painful subject. Every life is precious and cherished, yet some perspective beyond "if it bleeds, it leads" sensationalist journalism and the howls of peacenik movements is mandatory. About 140 miles west of Philadelphia, 51,000 American soldiers died in a three-day battle in July 1863 at Gettysburg. Some 2,400 Allied men died on D-Day (June 6, 1944) and another 7,900 were wounded; more than 6,500 Marines and 21,000 Japanese soldiers died in five weeks on Iwo Jima; the 82-day battle of Okinawa cost more lives (about a quarter of a million) than were lost through both atomic bombs dropped on Japan – one reason these horrific weapons were used to end the war. The great 1950 Chosin Reservoir seventy-mile fighting retreat from entrapment by 100,000 Chinese troops cost 3,400 American (the 1st Marine Division and the 7th Infantry Division) and more than 25,000 Chinese soldiers' lives during 18 days of combat. But it helped secure democracy in South Korea for the next sixty years, where it still thrives. That war is hell is more than merely a cliché. The 2,600 American military dead in the first three years in Iraq is grievous cost, to be sure, and in no way to be minimized. But it doesn't compare with troop losses suffered in many of our previous military actions.[4]

8. Conclusion

If we can't "afford" the Bush policy, what can we afford? What's your plan? Is there an Obama policy? World politics is not like a

4. Cf. Karl Rove, *Courage and Consequence: My Life as a Conservative in the Fight* (New York: Threshold Editions, 2010), esp. chaps. 16 and 21.

philosophy seminar or a college debate – all hypothetical or just for fun. Something has to happen, something has to be *done* – right or wrong – sometimes with life or death consequences. Not long after U.S. Secretary of State Dean Rusk retired from office to become a law professor at the University of Georgia, I heard him say: *"At last I can have an opinion!"*

Walter Bagehot once sniffily complained that the United States government under the Constitution is all sail and no anchor. Well, however that may be, the wind is surely at our backs, and the sail is up. But let's just remember that politics is a pragmatic endeavor and not a suicide pact.

5. Eric Voegelin as Master Teacher

Notes for a Talk

1. Voegelin presented himself as someone who knew his business and based on a solid conviction that Greek philosophy is the foundation of political science. The lecture materials were presented from this coherent starting point.

2. Devotion to truth and a desire to communicate it to students illumined every lecture and discussion, with the exploration of questions constantly reflecting the tension toward the divine Ground of reality as the decisive context for exploring the human condition and political issues.

3. This sense of openness to the horizon of being, and refusal to truncate reality or go along with reductionist constructs of any kind whatever, encouraged students to engage in the examination of complicated materials as partners in the discussion – rather than as mere auditors absorbing information.

4. This, in turn, encouraged students sympathetically to involve their own common sense, intellectual, and faith experiences in understanding demanding material in personal reflective consciousness, somewhat on the pattern of the Socratic "Look and see if this is not the case" – i.e., by validating the analytical discourse through personal critical understanding and questioning.

5. To this degree Voegelin was doing *science* as he taught, whether in lecture or in seminar – and everybody knew this is what we were doing. The students and class were to a

greater or lesser degree participants in a persuasive inquiry, in something appreciated as a search for truth, for truth that mattered! I think this palpable sense of participation in the activity of inquiry was perhaps the chief source of Voegelin's popularity as a teacher. It radiated respect for his students.

6.   Understood in this way, it becomes clear that *teaching* lies quite close to the center of much of Voegelin's scholarly work, whether published or communicated in lectures far and wide. And it is noteworthy that he never declined an invitation to speak: Ask him and he'd accept, if at all possible.

7.   As he said in a talk in 1972: "The foundation of [the Political Science Institute in Munich] offered the opportunity to establish political science, from the outset, on the level of contemporary science. One could avoid the conventional ballast of descriptive institutionalism, historical positivism, as well as of the various leftist and rightist ideological opinions . . . [I]t was possible to build a curriculum that had at its center the courses and seminars in classical politics and Anglo-American politics (with the stresses on Locke and the *Federalist Papers*)"[1]

8.   Voegelin's teaching method managed to communicate the meditative grounding of his thought. *GOD* was not a dirty word. He often stressed to his secular-minded audiences (especially in Munich) that *science* is controlled by *experience* – and you can't go back of revelation, ignore the occasions when it occurred, or pretend that such pneumatic experiences never happened. This basis of *faith* was more firmly in place in America, especially in Louisiana, where he

1.   Eric Voegelin, *The Drama of Humanity and Other Miscellaneous Papers, 1939–1985,* ed. William Petropulos and Gilbert Weiss (Columbia: University of Missouri Press, 2004), 348, vol. 33 of *The Collected Works of Eric Voegelin,* 34 vols.

taught for sixteen years. He was always telling the "saving tale of immortality" in a variety of ways – out of a conviction that the experience of transcendence is essential to man's existence as human. This was not argued "religiously" or blandly assumed but buttressed scientifically through the facts of experience grounded in a powerful theory of consciousness. Thus, a *professor* is expected to profess *truth*, as far as he knows it, he thought.

9.   He effectively used chalkboard diagrams in lecture, and there was generally an engaging undertone of playful levity that was Socratic in spirit. We are dealing with important matters, he would occasionally remark, but what we are doing with them here may not very important.

10.   Voegelin was a scourge to slothful ignoramuses: "I have always had to explain to the students at the beginning of my seminars all my life: There is no such thing as a right to be stupid; there is no such thing as a right to be illiterate; there is no such thing as a right to be incompetent."[2] And God help you if you were a faculty member and didn't know what you were talking about!

2.   Ibid., 419.

6. What Is a Mystic Philosopher and Why It Matters

A Note on Voegelin's Political Theory

The question posed by the title, addressed in Eric Voegelin's work and central to it, can be answered briefly: A mystic philosopher is one who takes the tension toward the transcendent divine Ground of being as the cardinal attribute of human reality per se and explores the whole hierarchy of being from this decisive perspective. Thus, all philosophy worthy of the name is mystic philosophy. It has been so from the pre-Socratics to Plato to Voegelin himself, by his account, as the *sine qua non* of philosophizing, past, present, and future. It *matters* because more than a mere definition is at stake. It matters because the experiential core of noetic and pneumatic reality, insofar as glimpsed in consciousness and regarded as basic to human existence, is available only through individual persons' divine-human mystical encounters – which happen as events in a variety of modalities evidenced from prehistory to the present. As Voegelin makes the point:

> The philosophical process never begins with the categories of being but, as with every important thinker, with the rationalization of the experiences of God by means of the mystical *via negativa*. I have worked this out with examples from the *Upanishads*, Plato's *Symposium*, Plotinus' *Enneads*, the book on time and memory in Augustine's *Confessions*, and Descartes' *Meditations*. Compared to the *via negativa*, I think the chain of being is a secondary phenomenon.[1]

1. Voegelin to Friedrich Engel-Janosi, Feb. 1, 1943, letter 166 in *Selected Correspondence, 1924–1949*, trans. William Petropulos, ed. and intro.

If it be suspected that this implies that the textbook version of the history of philosophy may be in largest part the history of its derailment, the point is conceded, as Voegelin himself tells us.[2] To inventory and critique the assorted ways in which the philosophic impulse has been diverted or has otherwise gone astray is a task for another day – a task, however, already substantially addressed in Voegelin's own life-long quest for truth in resistance to untruth under such familiar rubrics as sophistry, gnosticism, Scholasticism, Enlightenment, phenomenalism, ideology, scientism, and positivism, among myriad other deformations. Enough in this note if I can bring a bit more clearly to light the meaning and implications of mystic philosophy and its importance for a non-reductionist exploration of metaxic reality, one grounded in common sense and participatory (or apperceptive) empiricism –i.e., one that invokes in principle the Socratic "Look and see if this is not the case."

This then gets us to more familiar ground: Mystic philosophy is what Plato's Socrates was about, as the messenger of the God. Sundry Spinozaists and latter-day Averroists among us will be unpersuaded, since for them and their epigones, theology (a neologism and term of art in Plato, *Republic* 379a) and philosophy are adamantly asserted to be radically different enterprises.[3] However, to argue that the history of philosophy is largely the history of its

Jürgen Gebhardt (Columbia: University of Missouri Press, 2009), 354, vol. 29 of *The Collected Works of Eric Voegelin*, 34 vols (hereinafter, *CW*).

2. Cf. Eric Voegelin, *Order and History*, 5 vols. (Baton Rouge: Louisiana State University Press, 1956–1987), 3:277. This original edition has been re-edited and published as *CW* 14–18.

3. "Between faith or theology, and philosophy, there is no connection. . . . Philosophy has no end in view save truth; faith . . . looks for nothing but obedience and piety. Again, philosophy is based on axioms which must be sought from nature alone." Benedict de Spinoza, *Tractatus theologico-politicus* [1670], in *Writings on Political Philosophy*, ed. A. G. A. Balz, trans. R. H. M. Elwes (New York: Appleton-Century-Crofts, 1937), 16. Related issues are explored in "Medieval Rationalism or Mystic Philosophy? The Strauss-Voegelin Debate," chap. 6 of *Republicanism, Religion, and the Soul of America*, by Ellis Sandoz (Columbia: University of Missouri Press, 2006), 121–44.

derailment admittedly puts Voegelin somewhat in the company of Johannes Brahms when he supposedly departed a social gathering, insouciantly turning at the door to say, "If there's anyone here I haven't offended, I apologize."

What is at stake here, however, is more than social amenities. When Voegelin told an old friend from their Vienna days not to be too surprised to learn that he was a *mystic* as well as a philosopher,[4] he did so after a high-stakes battle to recover something of the truth of reality – one he had pursued for decades so as to find his way out of the lethal quandaries of radical modernity and convincingly critique National Socialism. The effort produced three books while he was a professor in Vienna and cost him his job – and very nearly his life.[5] Still, as the battle in various less grim forums continued thereafter, humor intruded from time to time. So it was with a genial intramural debate while at LSU in the 1940s with the head of the philosophy department (a great admirer of Bertrand Russell) that at one point supposedly found Voegelin retorting to this effect: Mr. Carmichael you are a philosophy professor. I am a philosopher.[6]

---

4. Saint "Thomas [Aquinas] is a mystic, for he knows that behind the God of dogmatic theology there is the tetragrammatic abyss that lies even behind the *analogia entis*. But in that sense also Plato is mystic, for he knows that behind the gods of the Myth, and even behind the Demiurge of his philosophy, there is the real God about whom one can say nothing. It may horrify you: But when somebody says that I am a mystic, I am afraid I cannot deny it. My enterprise of what you call 'de-reification' would not be possible, unless I were a mystic." Voegelin to Gregor Sebba, Feb. 3, 1973, letter 422 in *CW* 30, *Selected Correspondence, 1950–1984*, trans. Sandy Adler, Thomas A. Hollweck, and William Petropulos, ed. and intro. Thomas A. Hollweck (Columbia: University of Missouri Press, 2007), 751.

5. The books were published in 1933 and in 1938 in Germany and in Austria. For particulars, see the English translations and editors' introductions in *CW* 2, 3, and 5: *Race and State; The History of the Race Idea;* and *Political Religions*, respectively. For details, see Eric Voegelin, *Autobiographical Reflections*, ed. and intro. Ellis Sandoz, rev. ed. with glossary (Columbia: University of Missouri Press, 2011), 73–83.

6. Peter Carmichael remained a friend, as can be seen from a public letter he wrote, reprinted in *Eric Voegelin in Baton Rouge*, by Monika Puhl (Munich: Wilhelm Fink Verlag, 2005), 141–42.

Voegelin gave perhaps the fullest direct clarification of the pertinent issues in a 1965 talk to the German Political Science Association plenary session, subsequently published as "What Is Political Reality?"[7] The drift of that presentation is to explain why political science cannot rightly be assimilated to the natural science model most famously exemplified by Newton's *Principia Mathematica* but has its own unique paradigm as a *philosophical* science, which Voegelin sketches on the occasion. In effect it was a minority report to political scholars eager, then as now, to be as "scientific" as possible; thus the tenor is combative as well as diagnostic and therapeutic.

Selected Texts

1.   "Whoever has had enough of rebellion against the ground and wishes again to think rationally needs only to turn around and toward that reality against which the symbols of rebellion aggress."[8]

2.   "The classical noesis and mysticism are the two predogmatic realities of knowledge in which the logos of consciousness was differentiated in a paradigmatic way."[9]

3.   "Noetic exegesis differentiates the *ratio* as the material structure of consciousness. . . . Noesis frees the structure of the world in a radical way by removing mythical, revelatory, ideological, and other mortgages on truth. . . . Our study set out from the classical noesis but went considerably further."[10]

---

7.   Eric Voegelin, *Anamnesis*, trans. and ed. Gerhart Niemeyer (Columbia: University of Missouri Press, 1978), 143–214; originally Voegelin, *Anamnesis: Zur Theorie der Geschichte und Politik* (Munich: R. Piper & Co. Verlag, 1966); also revised and reprinted in CW 6, trans. M. J. Hanak, ed. and intro. David Walsh (2002).
8.   Voegelin, *Anamnesis*, ed. Niemeyer, 188.
9.   Ibid., 192.
10.   Ibid., 206: "[W]e . . . need a more differentiated language than that of clas-

4.   "The *realm of man* is not an object of empirical perception but a function of the participating consciousness. . . . The existential tension toward the ground is man's center of order."[11]

5.   "There are no principles of political science . . . [rather there are] commonsense insights into correct modes of action concerning man's existence in society. . . . If we go beyond the commonsense level we get to the insights into the order of consciousness [achieved through noesis]. . . . The insights of noesis owe their 'height' not to their generality but to the level of the participating consciousness in the hierarchy of levels of being. The existential tension toward the ground orders the entire existence of man, the corporeal foundation included."[12]

Commentary

The understanding of *experience* as participatory is key. The core is in common sense apprehension, especially of love, goodness, and beauty. Thus, Voegelin does not analytically drive the wedge of experience between the reality experienced and our consciousness of it as discrete elements of the act of knowing, as is usual with the intentionality of thing-knowledge. He avoids this by showing *participatory* experience to be a different mode from sensory experience, thereby rejecting the model of apprehension of things as entities in favor of the mutuality of tensional relationship. To communicate this he sometimes resorts to various hyphenated signs, such as experience-symbolization, divine-human, etc., as characteristic of the *metaxy,* or In-Between reality,

sical philosophy. No longer can we speak, without qualification, of 'human nature,' 'the nature of society,' or of 'the essence of history'. . . . Noetic experience . . . brings into view the relations between the ground of being and man, ground of being and world, . . . so that [today] the reality-image of being replaces the reality-image of the cosmic primary experience."
11. Ibid., 207–8.
12. Ibid., 210–11.

where noetic and pneumatic knowledge is luminosity rather than the discernment of discrete entities as with thing-knowledge. Nor does Voegelin identify the consciousness of the human speculator with the reality of which he is conscious, as with Hegel.[13] Rather, he preserves the paradoxical tension of knower and known even in the mutuality of participatory awareness and luminosity, which he signals as "reflective distance" while also acknowledging "There is something in the structure of consciousness-reality-language that forces us to think in the mode of thingness," even after noesis differentiates It-reality and thing-reality.[14] The participatory relationship itself extends to the penetration of *things* by the divine: We have no experience of an absolutely natural *nature*, i.e., of a realm wholly isolated from grace. Moreover, even our flawed knowledge of reality can only be expressed in flawed language grounded in thingness, where nonthings are represented as things.

Voegelin's primary concern is with the structure-process of reality, and on occasion he characterizes *Order and History* itself as an ontology.[15] However, he repeatedly underlines his insistence on *concreteness* and shows his wariness of every abstraction and classification. He avoids hermeneutics no less than dialectics, especially in the late work, so as to stay close to reality-experienced-symbolized. Thus, there is no "human consciousness" that differentiates. Rather, there is *only* the consciousness of individual human beings who from time to time uniquely respond to divine initiatives or irruptions. A collaborative divine-human quest for

13. Cf. Voegelin, "On Hegel: A Study in Sorcery," in *CW* 12, *Published Essays, 1966–1985*, ed. and intro. Ellis Sandoz (Baton Rouge: Louisiana State University Press, 1990), 213–55.
14. Eric Voegelin, *Order and History*, vol. 5, *In Search of Order* (Baton Rouge: Louisiana State University Press, 1987), 100. (Hereinafter, *OH5*. Abbreviations of other *Order and History* volumes will follow the same format on second and subsequent references.). Cf. Ellis Sandoz, *The Voegelinian Revolution: A Biographical Introduction*, 2nd ed. (1981; repr. New Brunswick: Transaction Pubs., 2000), esp. chap. 7, "*Principia Noetica*," 143–87, and the epilogue, 253–77.
15. "It is an ontology of social order and history." Letter to Carl J. Friedrich, April 12, 1959, letter 180 in *CW* 30:388.

truth thereby differentiates the reality of which individual persons are self-reflective members, and the new insights are propagated through persuasion in their various communities.[16] The celebrated "leap in being" or pivotal differentiating experience of millennial significance – disclosing the soul to be the sensorium of transcendence and transcendent divine Being as hegemonic reality in several modes and in different ethnic horizons – illustrates the dynamic and its limitations. But it is as ubiquitous as individual noetic or pneumatic conversion (*periagoge, epistrophe, conversio*), personal vocation, and every insight into the truth of existence at whatever level attained.[17]

Voegelin is emphatic that all tiers of the hierarchy of being are interdependent. There can be no good life without life itself, and neither man, society, nor history exists apart from corporeal foundations: Kill the body and you destroy the human existent, who, metaphysical quibbles aside, is silently left in death to the hope of eternal salvation through faith.[18] The anchoring of human

16. Cf. "In Search of the Ground" in *CW* 11, *Published Essays, 1953–1965*, ed. and intro. Ellis Sandoz (Columbia: University of Missouri Press, 2000), 243. Cited and discussed in Thomas A. Hollweck, "Cosmos and the 'Leap in Being' in Voegelin's Philosophy," paper delivered at the 2010 Eric Voegelin Society meeting, at n33. The point is eloquently made in *CW* 31, *Hitler and the Germans*, trans., ed., and intro. Detlev Clemens and Brendan Purcell (Columbia: University of Missouri Press, 1999), 205–9: "These insights occur in determinate men, who, again, are in determinate societies. . . . Very often they are ineffective even within the bounds of this society, for the one who is immediately understanding is always only one individual human being, and whether he is a prophet or a philosopher makes no difference" (205). This singularity, it may be noted, has striking physiological analogy in the uniqueness of individual fingerprints, facial identifying characteristics, and DNA.

17. Cf. Ellis Sandoz, "The Philosopher's Vocation: The Voegelinian Paradigm," *Review of Politics* 71 (2009): 54–67.

18. Philosophical anthropology may be consulted in this connection, from Plato onward the heart of political theory. In one powerful medieval formulation: "[T]here is a soul in the child which hath vegetative power in actual exercise, since the child groweth; he hath also a percipient power in actual exercise, since the child feeleth; he hath moreover an imaginative power, but not yet in actual exercise; and a reasoning power, the exercise whereof is as yet

personality and of overall reality in the unique *physical* existence of each and every *individual man and woman* is the self-evident warrant of the ineradicable worth and dignity of even the least of these as bearers of *imago Dei.* The insight has special pungency in our effete age of complacently dehumanizing man in the name of man doctrinally. The blatant factual consequence is rampant murderous destruction of millions of human beings on biological, social class, religious, or other dogmatic pretexts – perhaps most easily when individual human beings are discounted as mere nodal points gathering together the sum total of social relationships (Marx) – killing merely for "the fun of it."[19] The totalitarian killers come into view, and politics is seen to be more than a harmless intellectual game. Voegelin writes by way of contrast:

> Through the seeking for the divine, the loving reaching out beyond ourselves toward the divine in the philosophical experience and the loving encounter through the Word in the pneumatic experience, man participates in the divine. . . . Insofar as man shares in the divine, insofar, that is to say, as he can experience it, man is "theomorphic," in the Greek term, or the image of God, the *imago Dei,* in the pneumatic

still more remote; he hath, too, an intellectual power, but that is even more delayed in developing. Thus we find that one and the same soul hath the lower powers in actual exercise first, and afterward the higher, as if man were animal before he is spiritual. . . . Draw me, Lord, for none can come unto Thee save he be drawn by Thee; grant that, thus drawn, I may be set free from this world and may be united unto Thee, the absolute God, in an eternity of glorious life. Amen." Nicholas of Cusa, *The Vision of God* [1453], trans. Emma Gurney Salter (Escondido, CA: The Book Tree, 1999), 120–21, 130. For the hierarchy of being from *Nous* to *Apeiron* and its theory, see the important synopsis, diagram, and discussion in the appendix to Voegelin, "Reason: The Classic Experience," in *Anamnesis,* ed. Niemeyer, 114–15; also reprinted in *CW* 12:289–91. Cf. also "The Gospel and Culture," in *CW* 12:172–212. For Voegelin's analysis of Nicholas of Cusa, see *CW* 21, *History of Political Ideas,* vol. 3, *The Later Middle Ages,* ed. and intro. David Walsh (Columbia: University of Missouri Press, 1998), 256–66.

19. Voegelin, *Autobiographical Reflections,* ed. Sandoz, chap. 14, p. 74. The Marx text occurs in *Theses on Feuerbach.*

sphere. The specific dignity of man is based on this. . . .[20] Unfolding at the level of the questing meditative's open ascent to the vision of God – the infinite flowing Presence of the ineffable It-reality beyond symbolization-experience –, ambiguity, paradox, and silence attend the process whereby the ineffable somehow becomes effable in human experience.[21] All representation falters as the symbols partake of the ineffable mystery of infinitude to yield only such enigmatic linguistic markers of the quest as the Parmenidean *IS!* or Mosaic *I AM* or Platonic *GOOD* beyond being – and we are otherwise left in silence.[22]

Following Jean Bodin and Pseudo-Dionysius, along with Henri Bergson and Plotinus, Voegelin stresses the inadequacy of all symbolization to express the reality of knowing participation. "Behind the knowledge, which enters into the symbol, there is always the ineffability of the knowledge about the inexhaustibility of the

---

20. Voegelin, *Anamnesis*, ed. Niemeyer, 210; quotation from *Hitler and the Germans*, CW 31:87.
21. Voegelin, *OH5*:103: "When the paradoxic experience of not-experientiable reality becomes conscious in reflective distance [in Plato], the questioner's language reveals itself as the paradoxic event of the ineffable becoming effable. This tension of effable-ineffable is the paradox in the structure of meditative language that cannot be dissolved by a speculative meta-language of the kind by which Hegel wanted to dissolve the paradoxic 'identity of identity and non-identity.' In reflective distance, the questioner rather experiences his speech as the divine silence breaking creatively forth in the imaginative word that will illuminate the quest as the questioner's movement of return to the ineffable silence. The quest, thus, has no external 'object,' but is reality itself becoming luminous for its movement from the ineffable, through the Cosmos, to the ineffable."
22. Cf. Voegelin, *Order and History,* vol. 2, *The World of the Polis* (Baton Rouge; Louisiana State University Press, 1957), 211: "[Parmenides's] progress on the way toward the Light culminates in an experience of a supreme reality that can only be expressed in the exclamatory 'Is!'" See Voegelin's important later analysis of Parmenides in *OH5*:86–90. For a comparable analysis of exploration of nonexistent reality in the medieval context, see Fran O'Rourke, *Pseudo-Dionysius and the Metaphysics of Aquinas* (1992; repr. Notre Dame: University of Notre Dame Press, 2005), chap. 7, §"Aquinas and the Good beyond Being," pp. 201–12 and passim.

ground. . . . Symbolism is no more than the last word of each historical religion; the reality of faith through *conversio* lies beyond the symbols."[23] One possible *prudential* consequence, as Bodin taught, is (or ought to be: Fanaticism is so much more enjoyable, as we still see today!) the moderation of raging dogmatomachy or warfare of contending dogmas through the balm of religious and political *toleration*: The ultimate truth of *faith* is not at stake in the dogmas or even in the symbols. At the contemplative level we are reminded of the radical inadequacy of *all* experience-symbolization. This is emphasized in later paradoxic formulations, such as: "Even when the divine Beyond reveals itself in its formative presence, it remains the unrevealed divine reality beyond its revelation."[24]

Conclusion

Questions remain, of course, but these hints will perhaps suffice to secure the chief points of analysis for present purposes and even to stir further interest in the issues. The open quest of the process of reality for its truth (for which Anselm's *fides quaerens intellectum* is taken to be paradigmatic)[25] does not deliver a truth to end all truth. Rather, it signals the enduring *mystery* of being whose penetration by the responsive human being is precious but remains forever imperfect, ultimately "penultimate" in Voegelin's expression: The philosopher does not know and knows why he does not know. Philosophy, despite its limitations, nonetheless stands as an indispensable bulwark of noetic truth. It stands against reductionist manipulators and apocalyptic dreamers of all stripes whose lust for power in the warfare of contending dogmas often is unrestrained by any concern for *salus populi,* the

---

23. Voegelin, *Anamnesis*, ed. Niemeyer, 195, 197.
24. Voegelin, OH5:97.
25. Voegelin, "Quod Deus Dicitur," in CW 12:376–94, at 383: "Behind the quest, and behind the *fides* the quest is supposed to understand, there now becomes visible the true source of the Anselmian effort in the living desire of the soul to move toward the divine Light."

cornerstone of just governance, and for the well-being of every person in their respective communities. For while the physical safety of a society may be the cardinal political priority, the spiritual health nurtured by truth and justice in the public order and civic consciousness is essential to the happiness of individuals and to the thriving of the societies they compose. This is not a novel insight, but unoriginal thinking may bear the mark of truth in human affairs. As Voegelin writes:

> The philosopher's way is the way up toward the light, not the way down into the cave. . . . The search for truth makes sense only under the assumption that the truth brought up from the depth of his psyche by [one] man, though it is not the ultimate truth of reality, is representative of the truth in the divine depth of the Cosmos. . . . The search that renders no more than equivalent truth rests ultimately on the faith that, by engaging in it, [a] man participates representatively in the divine drama of truth becoming luminous.[26]

The beginning of mystic philosophy (i.e., of philosophy per se), in Parmenides's differentiation of being, and the discovery of *Nous* and *logos* also was accompanied by the differentiation of the individual soul in its search for the truth of being. Mystic philosophy was thereby born in a responsive movement in Hellas akin to the one reflected in the "Suffering Servant" (Isa. 52–53) of Deutero-Isaiah in Israel. Parmenides's poem *Way of Truth* (ca. 485 B.C.) experientially gives his mystical vision of being (*Eon*) and personal immortality. Voegelin writes:

> Only with Jesus does the symbol of the Way of Truth appear in the Jewish orbit. But when Jesus answers the question of the apostle with his "I am the way, the truth, and the life" (John 14:6), he firmly takes the symbol away from the philosophers. From then onward the redemption of the soul goes through Christ; the component of redemption, which is

---

26. Voegelin, "Equivalences of Experience and Symbolization in History" in *CW* 12:119, 122, 133.

still present in the compact philosophizing of Parmenides, has been revealed in its true meaning; and philosophy, the sole source of transcendent order for the polis, has become one of the two sources of order for mankind, that of Reason by the side of Revelation.[27]

If one is finally left wondering what the individual must *do* in order to propagate truth and to resist massive societal corruption as a personal obligation, Voegelin invokes personal responsibility and is fond of quoting God's message to the prophet Ezekiel – a passage he told the students to memorize:

> So you, son of man, I have made a watchman for the house of Israel; whenever you hear a word from my mouth, you shall give them warning from me. If I say to the wicked, O wicked man, you shall surely die, and you do not speak to warn the wicked to turn from his way, that wicked man shall die in his iniquity, but his blood I will require at your hand. But if you warn the wicked to turn from his way, and he does not turn from his way; he shall die in his iniquity, but you will have saved your life.[28]

Life is lived not only in the present but in divine *Presence*, thus under Judgment.[29] Every individual is obliged to seek truth and live in accordance with it, to resist evil, live his life in order and –

27. Voegelin, *OH*2:203–4; cf. 207–14 passim.
28. Ezek. 33:7–9 [RSV] as in *Hitler and the Germans, CW* 31:200. The passage also is quoted at the end of Voegelin, "The German University and the Order of German Society: A Reconsideration of the Nazi Era," in *CW* 12:1–35, at 35.
29. *Hitler and the Germans, CW* 31:71; cf. "flowing Presence" in Voegelin, "Eternal Being in Time," *Anamnesis,* chap.7, §2. Also *Order and History,* vol. 3, *Plato and Aristotle* (Baton Rouge: Louisiana State University Press, 1957), chap. 2, §5, The Judgment of the Dead, 39–45, and chap. 3, §6, dealing with *techne metretike,* 129–34, and life lived *sub specie mortis.* "The real importance of the 'art of measurement' must have consisted in its application to the long-range perspectives, and especially to the longest of all, that is, to the whole of life that ends in death. . . . [Thus] the distortions of time were meant to be corrected by the love of the measure that is out of time." *OH*2:291.

as far as he is able to do it – not succumb to corruptions prevalent in society, regardless of the sources.[30] The philosopher, like the prophets of old, Voegelin insists, is thereby *called* to represent truth and order in his society and to be a rallying point of representative authority. This is most especially true in times of crisis when the public institutions are perverted, abandon their obligation to justice and truth, and fail by becoming tyrannical – i.e., mere coercive instruments of *libido dominandi*. Thus the aptness of the Ezekiel passage with its invocation of the Watchman, the man called to serve Truth and answerable for his conduct to the eternal God, who ever abides as Judge and divine Measure.[31]

30. For a summary analysis of corruption see *OH3*:78–80.
31. Cf. the discussion of this theme in Sandoz, "The Philosopher's Vocation," passim.

7. Mysticism and Politics
in Voegelin's Philosophy

By Voegelin's account, the philosopher's vocation is to love the Good, to serve the truth of Being in its highest dimensions, to live in attunement with it, and to resist untruth. The worldwide contemporary assault on truth Voegelin saw as a revolt of unique scope against the divine ground of being. Since he admittedly philosophized in response to the political situation, the core of his resistance lay in the affirmation of the truth of being in response to specific political threats to it.

When asked toward the end of our interviews, in what became *Autobiographical Reflections,* the "So what?" question of "Why philosophize?" his answer was, "To recapture reality."[1] By this he especially meant highest reality glimpsed through experience as most notably articulated in the differentiated noetic and pneumatic modes lying at the core of the contemplative's meditative process. As he stressed from time to time, reality remains what it is and what it will be. Not God but man is perplexed, ever wandering in mazes lost, proclaiming the death of God and nervously acting on the perplexity like Ivan Karamazov's Grand Inquisitor in bidding Christ never to come again – doubtless to God's own amusement, the only One permitted to laugh, a thought akin to Solzhenitsyn's sly observation that Buddha smiled.[2]

1. Voegelin, *Autobiographical Reflections,* ed. and intro. Ellis Sandoz (Columbia: University of Missouri Press, 2006), 120, vol. 34 of *The Collected Works of Eric Voegelin,* 34 vols. (hereinafter, *CW*); also issued separately as Eric Voegelin, *Autobiographical Reflections,* ed. and intro. Ellis Sandoz, rev. ed. with glossary (Columbia: University of Missouri Press, 2011), same pagination.
2. Cf. Voegelin, *Order and History,* vol. 5, *In Search of Order,* ed. and intro. Ellis Sandoz (Columbia: University of Missouri Press, 2000), chap. 2,

Resistance and remediation therefore frame a high-stakes *political* game. They force the philosopher to find intellectual footing in the deepest sources of spiritual sustenance implicating ontology and anthropology, the ineffable Reality made effable through human experience in the representative work of the great contemplatives.[3] Reductionist materialism of the positivist, National Socialist, or communist kinds – including biologism, economism, and scientism in all its other guises – appears politically as armed ideological movements claiming exclusive truth and usurping reality for themselves. In the face of this array of power, evil, and distortion, the recourse of the resisting individual person, as with Ezekiel's Watchman long ago, can only be to the eminent Reality transcending time and history, the Divine *Presence* within which the human drama turgidly plays out in day-to-day existence, in politics, and in the broad reach of history.

Thus Voegelin's appeals to the great mystics. Among them: first to Augustine,[4] then to Thomas à Kempis at the beginning

§2.14., p. 83, vol. 18 of *The Collected Works of Eric Voegelin*, 34 vols. (hereinafter, *CW*). For Grand Inquisitor, see Ellis Sandoz, *Political Apocalypse A Study of Dostoevsky's Grand Inquisitor*, 2nd ed. (Wilmington, DE: ISI Books, 2000), 126 and passim. For "Buddha's Smile," see Solzhenitsyn, *The First Circle*, trans. Thomas P. Whitney (New York: Bantam Books, 1981), chap. 54. Voegelin's resistance is defiant; thus he writes: "The order of being itself [ever remains] utterly unchanged. Even if Hegel, Marx, and Nietzsche thoroughly murder God and explain him away as dead, divine being remains eternal and man must still get on with living his life sealed by his creatureliness and by death." *CW* 31, *Hitler and the Germans,* trans., ed., and intro. Detlev Clemens and Brendan Purcell (Columbia: University of Missouri Press, 1999), 262.

3. This is a matter of great delicacy. Thus, Voegelin writes: "When the paradoxic experience of not-experientiable reality becomes conscious in reflective distance, the questioner's language reveals itself as the paradoxic event of the ineffable becoming effable." *CW* 18:119–20. See also Voegelin, "The German University and the Order of German Society: A Reconsideration of the Nazi Era," in *CW* 12, *Published Essays 1966–1985,* ed. and intro. Ellis Sandoz (Baton Rouge: Louisiana State University Press, 1990), 1–35.

4. Voegelin, "Notes on Augustine: Time and Memory," in *CW* 32, *The Theory of Governance and Other Miscellaneous Papers, 1921–1938,* ed. and intro. William Petropulos and Gilbert Weiss (Columbia: University of Missouri Press, 2003), 483–501.

of *The History of the Race Idea,* for instance; to the anonymous meditative called the Frankfurter as author of the *German Theology* at the end of *Political Religions;* and finally to Anselm of Canterbury's *Proslogion.* Therein lies the culmination of Voegelin's quest to find a satisfactory paradigm of philosophizing by determining the limits of *sapientia experimentalis,* or felt presence of God, emerging in fragmentary fashion into articulate *knowledge* in noetic-pneumatic exegesis as the fruition of the meditative's open search of the metaxic divine-human reality for its truth. The mentioned illustrative way stations in Voegelin's pilgrimage seeking illumination of the It-Reality are thus dated at ca. 1931, 1933, 1938, and 1985. But these dates merely indicate the continuity in a reflective life that can be traced from the earliest writings, one sustained with great consistency down to the deathbed meditation, "Quod Deus Dicitur," of January 1985.[5] The continuity rests on his insight that the key problem of philosophy is the relation to transcendence, i.e., that philosophy originates in mysticism. I shall merely recall here a few elements from extensive material for consideration.

Faced in 1933 with the experience that the knowledge of man had come to grief in a world palpably infested with blackest evil, Voegelin at the outset, almost in the spirit of the exorcist, defiantly invokes the anthropology of *The Imitation of Christ* against the bestial reduction of human being to cranial indexes and pseudo-scientific racial phenomenal traits. It is man as *imago Dei,* the image of God, he offers in blistering response in the first pages of

---

5. Voegelin, "Quod Deus Dicitur," in *CW* 12:376–94. "The question raised by the title of this lecture has received its specific form through Thomas Aquinas in his *Summa Theologiae* 1.2.3." First sentence, ibid., 376. Also Voegelin to Aron Gurwitsch, Aug. 27, 1949, letter 299 in *CW* 29, *Selected Correspondence, 1924–1949,* trans. William Petropulos, ed. and intro. Jürgen Gebhardt (Columbia: University of Missouri Press, 2009), 645: "He [Harry Wolfson] simply does not respond to the profound issue of philosophizing as a process of the soul and [investigate] the origins of the process and its motivations. Such a response would lead him to discover the origins of philosophizing in mysticism."

his own meticulous analysis, the "primal image"[6] immemorially preserved in human consciousness and experience but now shamelessly mutilated and debauched by a pretentious pseudo-biology arrogantly and ignorantly elevating the imaginary Aryan super race. Voegelin finds "originary meditation" by individual human beings to be the root of philosophizing, as in Augustine's *intentio* of the soul toward transcendence in the *Ungrund*.[7] There is mystical, i.e., spiritual and noetic, significance in the impetus provided from the *first* such experience in a chain or tradition – thus his emphasis on Anselm as the originator of Scholasticism. This is an elusive subject, implying Divine initiative (irruption) and a specific human being's response to it on each such occasion as seminal in both philosophy and revelation, thereby decisively structuring politics and history in the process.

God is, thus, definitely present and at work in human affairs, as Voegelin insists in a variety of subtle and not-so-subtle ways. The divine impetus is realized in time by responsive individual human beings as agency in a metaxic movement through finite thing-reality toward participatory fulfillment in the divine infinitude of transcendence. Of this metaxic reality Voegelin writes in 1933, quoting Thomas à Kempis:

> The Christian image raises man out of nature; though it presents him as a creature among other creatures, as a finite being among others, it nevertheless juxtaposes him to the rest of nature; he stands between God and the subhuman world. This intermediate status is not determined by a unique formative law that would constitute man as a self-contained

---

6. Voegelin, CW 3, *The History of the Race Idea :From Ray to Carus,* trans. Ruth Hein, ed. and intro. Klaus Vondung (Baton Rouge: Louisiana State University Press, 1998), 3–5.

7. Voegelin to Alfred Schütz, Sept. 17, 1943, in CW 29:377; Voegelin, "Notes on Augustine," in CW 32:497–501; Voegelin, "The Meditative Origin of the Philosophical Knowledge of Order," in CW 33, *The Drama of Humanity and Other Miscellaneous Papers, 1939–1985,* ed. and intro. William Petropulos and Gilbert Weiss (Columbia: University of Missouri Press, 2004), 384–95.

existence but by his participation in both the higher and the lower world. By virtue of his soul, man is united with the divine *pneuma*; by virtue of his body, his *sarx*, he partakes of transitoriness. . . . Man must live according to the example of Christ and follow Him: . . . "All is vanity but to love God, and to serve him alone. Thus the supreme wisdom is to seek the kingdom of heaven by despising the things of this world."[8]

Five years later in the conclusion of *Political Religions,* having studied and savored Nazi truth more completely and being fired as a professor from the University of Vienna, Voegelin reminds readers of the anonymous fourteenth-century mystic called the Frankfurter in counterpoint to the prevailing millenarian apocalypse of the newly ascendant Superman destined to perfect the world, whom he derides as satanic and later analyzes in terms of egophanic revolt. The point must be underlined: "As far as we Germans are concerned, he – the devil – seems to me to be so close to us that indeed we take him for God."[9] Again: "When considering National Socialism . . . one should be able to proceed on the assumption that there is evil in the world and, moreover, that evil is not only a deficient mode of being, a negative element, but also a real substance and force that is effective in the world. Resistance against a satanical substance that is not only morally but religiously evil can only be derived from an equally strong, religiously good

8. CW 3:4. The individual character or personal experience basic to the differentiations is stressed by Voegelin. "These insights occur in determinate men. . . in determinate societies. . . . [F]or the one who is immediately understanding is always only one individual human being, and whether he is a prophet or a philosopher makes no difference." CW 31:205. For the principal stages of differentiation first sketched in *The New Science of Politics* (Chicago: University of Chicago Press, 1952), chap. 3, as "three types of truth," see CW 5, *Modernity Without Restraint,* ed. and intro. Manfred Henningsen (Columbia: University of Missouri Press, 2000), 149–52 and passim.
9. Voegelin to Eduard Baumgarten, Sept. 13, 1936, letter 40 in CW 29:135. For egophanic revolt, see *Order and History,* vol. 4, *The Ecumenic Age,* CW 17, ed. and intro. Michael Franz (Columbia: University of Missouri Press, 2000), chap. 5, §2, pp. 326–32.

force. One cannot fight a satanical force with morality and human-ity alone."[10] As the Frankfurter had written centuries earlier:

> If the human creature attributes something good to itself . . . as if he were that or had that, as if it belonged to him or came from him, then he goes astray. What else did Satan do? What else was his fall and abandonment than his assumption that he were something too, and his wish to be someone and to have his own. This assumption and his "I" and "my," his "me" and "mine" were his abandonment and fall. And it is that way still.

To this Voegelin the political scientist energetically adds: "It is not indifferent how the sphere of human-political organization is inte-grated in the order of being. The inner-worldly religiosity experi-enced by the collective body – be it humanity, the people, the class, the race, or the state – as the *realissimum* is abandonment of God. . . . According to the *German Theology* the belief that man is the source of good and of improvement in the world, as it is held by the Enlightenment, and the belief that the collective body is a mys-terious, divine substance . . . is anti-Christian renunciation. . . . [T]he inner-worldly religiosity and its symbolism [of whatever kind] conceals the most essential parts of reality. It blocks the path to the reality of God and distorts the circumstances of the levels of being subordinate to God."[11]

The anthropology of the Christian mystics remains central in the *Hitler and the Germans* lectures of 1964 and in the subsequent lecture on the *German University* of the same year, where it is stressed that the human being is "theomorphic" and that his true destiny is potentially to enjoy the restoration of the *imago Dei*, mutilated in Adam, as the ultimate fulfillment of his spiritual and intellectual quest.[12]

10. CW 5:24, written in 1938 in the new preface to *Political Religions*; and the Frankfurter as quoted in the epilogue, p. 71.
11. CW 5:71.
12. "The German University and German Society," in CW 12:7; *Hitler and the Germans*, CW 31:86–87.

Finally, there is the approving exploration of the form of true philosophizing, arduously won by Anselm of Canterbury, as faith in search of understanding, and no less arduously pursued by Voegelin, until his effort finally plays out in the unfinished *In Search of Order.* He finds the structural *limits* of the noetic quest and conceptual analysis of man and, therewith, of human grandeur, cogently ascertained by Anselm and voiced in the prayerful exclamation of *Proslogion XV*:

> "O Lord, you are not only that than which a greater cannot be conceived but you are also greater than what can be conceived."

The contemplative's desiring heart, eagerly drawn toward the divine light in faith, now understands that the Light of It-reality yet far surpasses the noblest glimmerings attained by human beings through reason and vision. Experientially, Voegelin writes, "the divine reality lets the light of its perfection fall into the soul; the illumination of the soul arouses the awareness of man's existence as a state of imperfection; and this awareness provokes the human movement in response to the divine appeal. The illumination, as St. Augustine names this experience, has for Anselm indeed the character of an appeal, and even of a counsel and a promise."[13]

---

13. "Quod Deus Dicitur," in CW 12:383. To which Voegelin adds: "This is the limit of the noetic conceptual analysis disregarded by Hegel."

8. The Philosopher's Vocation:
The Voegelinian Paradigm

1. Introduction

In his personal and scholarly demeanor, Eric Voegelin's stance was overtly and explicitly that of a philosopher and teacher professing truth and resisting corruption. The mark of his life was intellectual integrity in the Weberian sense, and his only professional commitment was that of a partisan of truth. This was more than academic duty, however. It was quite distinctly a vocation – or *calling* (*klesis*)[1] – of the highest order and responsibility, one intrinsic to the paradigm of philosophizing Voegelin accepted from Plato and Anselm and differentiated in his own life and work. It is exemplified, directly evoked, in the "introduction to political science" he taught as a lecture course at the University of Munich in spring semester 1964, now published under the title *Hitler and the Germans*.[2] But it can

---

1. 2 Thess. 1:11 and 1 Pet. 2:9: "You are a ... . . . royal priesthood . . . that you should show forth the praises of him who has called you out of darkness into his marvelous light." Said of all believers under the dispensation of Grace who, living in immediacy to God, are sons of the heavenly Rex et Sacerdos. Cf. Rom 1:1–6, a passage Voegelin repeatedly read in his last days. It is a commonplace of Christian faith that "Conversion and vocation were for [St. Paul] one and the same event (Gal. 1:15–16)." Franz J. Leenhardt, *The Epistle to the Romans: A Commentary*, trans. Harold Knight (London: Lutterworth Press, 1961), 39.
2. *Hitler and the Germans*, trans., ed., and intro. Detlev Clemens and Brendan Purcell (Columbia: University of Missouri Press, 1999), vol. 31 of *The Collected Works of Eric Voegelin*, 34 vols. (hereinafter, *CW*). A German language edition of the course of lectures basic to the text of this book appeared as *Eric Voegelin, Hitler und die Deutschen*, ed. Manfred Henningsen (Munich: Wilhelm Fink Verlag, 2006). References herein are to the English language version unless otherwise indicated.

be traced everywhere in his writings, beginning in the 1930s, as a constant and defining attitude.[3] The implications are important not only for Voegelin but for philosophy itself when rightly done as embracing the science of human affairs palpably akin to that first elaborated in antiquity by Aristotle. It is this decisive, unfashionable, and somewhat elusive contextual dimension of *Hitler and the Germans* that I wish briefly to explore on the present occasion.

2. Calling and Authority

The responsive center of the philosopher's calling lies in the divine-human partnership, understood as participation in the process-structure governing metaxic-reality-experienced or "In-Between" – the only reality we have – with the philosopher cast in the role of representative man. The hyphenated terms are meant to symbolize as units of meaning the epistemologically *participatory* character of luminous meditative discourse, in contradistinction to the conventional intentionalist subject-object mode of propositional statements of doctrines about entities or things in the positivist reductionist mode of scientism addressing phenomenal experience of the external world.[4] Thus, Voegelin insists, the philosopher is a

3. As in the *Herrschaftslehre*, or theory of governance, chap. 1 on the "Concept of the Person," in CW 32, *The Theory of Governance and Other Miscellaneous Papers, 1921–1938*, ed. and intro. William Petropulos and Gilbert Weiss (Columbia: University of Missouri Press, 2003), 226–55.
4. For concise explanation of some of Voegelin's terminology, see the "Glossary of Terms Used in Eric Voegelin's Writings," in Voegelin, CW 34, *Autobiographical Reflections*, ed. and intro. Ellis Sandoz (Columbia: University of Missouri Press, 2006), 149–86, and the various indexes to the volumes in this edition, including the cumulative index; also Ellis Sandoz, *The Voegelinian Revolution: A Biographical Introduction*, 2nd ed. (1981; repr. New Brunswick: Transaction Pubs., 2000). Of the key "experience of transcendence" Voegelin writes: "The term *experience* [in this context] signifies an ontic event. It is a disturbance in being, an involvement of man with God by which the divine Within is revealed as the divine Beyond. What is achieved by it is immediacy of existence under God; what is discovered by it is the existence under God as the first principle of order for man. Moreover, the principle is discovered as valid not only for the man who has the experience but for every man, because the very idea of man arises from

lover of wisdom, never its possessor, for only God is wise and can have knowledge of the Whole. Political science is a prudential and noetic science. Thus, not the *natural* science of the external world, but *philosophical or noetic* science as perfected by Plato and Aristotle is paradigmatic for its inquiries into the order and disorders of the human condition. While largely a recovery and reinterpretation of the ancient "philosophy of human affairs," this is plainly political science in a new key to most contemporaries.[5] To make it intelligible and to find the way himself in resisting untruth, Voegelin expends substantial effort in working through the inadequacies of the still-prevailing positivist, Marxist, and other reductionist paradigms. That effort culminated at a provisional stage in the well-known conclusion that "the essence of modernity is Gnosticism."[6] In contrast to the overwhelming tendencies of

its realization in the presence under God. Both the reality and the idea of man are produced by the movement; the humanity represented is the humanity produced. In such terms can the *representative* character of the event be circumscribed." *CW* 28, *What Is History? and Other Late Unpublished Writings,* ed. and intro. Thomas A. Hollweck and Paul Caringella (Baton Rouge: Louisiana State University Press, 1990), 49 (italics added.) The theory of representation is the theme of Voegelin's first book in English, originally the 1951 Charles R. Walgreen Foundation Lectures at the University of Chicago, published as *The New Science of Politics: An Introduction* (Chicago: University of Chicago Press, 1952). A number of studies are available, including Barry Cooper, *Eric Voegelin and the Foundations of Modern Political Science* (Columbia: University of Missouri Press, 1999), and recently on Voegelin as mystic philosopher is Meins G. A. Coetsier, *Etty Hillesum and the Flow of Presence: A Voegelinian Analysis* (Columbia: University of Missouri Press, 2008), esp. chap. 3 and bibliography. The most comprehensive compilation of Voegeliniana is Geoffrey L. Price and Eberhard Freiherr von Lochner, eds., *Eric Voegelin: International Bibliography, 1921–2000* (Munich: Wilhelm Fink Verlag, 2000), supplemented by Peter J. Opitz, ed., *Voegeliniana Veröffentlichungen von und zu Eric Voegelin 2000–2005,* Occasional Papers 46, Jan. 2005 (Munich: Eric-Voegelin-Archiv, 2005).

5. Aristotle, *Nicomachean Ethics* 10.9.23, 1181b15–16; Voegelin, *The New Science of Politics,* 22–26, where the program of "restoration" and "reinterpretation" of rationalism in the wake of Gnostic ideological destruction is tentatively sketched.

6. Voegelin, *The New Science of Politics,* chap. 4; for the summary critique of positivism see the introduction, ibid., 2–22. Consequences of the argument

modernity, he argues, the philosopher's noesis (rational inquiry) is centered in his orienting tension toward the transcendent divine ground of being. It consists, constructively, in the exploration of philosophical anthropology as part of ontology that engages all the realms of the hierarchy of being from the Anaximandrian *apeiron* (depth) to the divine *Nous*, starting from common sense understanding and elaborated empirically through differentiating apperceptive experiences-symbolizations of the great spiritualists of all ages.[7] *Openness* to the Whole, experienced both noetically

are elaborated in Sandoz, "The Philosophical Science of Politics Beyond Behavioralism," in *The Post-Behavioral Era: Perspectives on Political Science*, ed. George J. Graham and George W. Carey (New York: David McKay, 1972), chap. 14. The substantive issues were pivotal for Voegelin's philosophical break with the neo-Kantianism of his teacher Hans Kelsen as given early on and definitively in *The New Science of Politics*, of which the latter wrote a book-length refutation that Voegelin responded to by letter: "There is no science which could develop a relevant concept of justice . . . [by] following the verification procedures of an immanent science. . . . The problem of justice is in my opinion not a problem of a normative science, or of a causal science, rather a problem of ontology." Voegelin to Hans Kelsen, March 7, 1954, letter 75 in CW 30, *Selected Correspondence, 1950–1984*, trans. Sandy Adler, Thomas A. Hollweck, and William Petropulos, ed. and intro. Thomas A. Hollweck (Columbia: University of Missouri Press, 2007), 217, 218. Cf. Voegelin, *Autobiographical Reflections*, CW 34, chap. 6, where it is said that the positivism of Hermann Cohen and the Marburg School defined "*science* [as] meaning Newton's physics as understood by Kant" (50). For the early (1936) detailed analysis of why this kind of science is wholly inadequate for a valid political science, see Voegelin, CW 4, *The Authoritarian State: An Essay on the Problem of the Austrian State*, trans. Ruth Hein, ed. and intro. Gilbert Weiss (Columbia: University of Missouri Press, 1999), historical commentary on the period by Erika Weinzierl, chap. 6, pp. 163–212. For the underlying philosophical problem of phenomenalism (including scientism), see the chapter of that title in Voegelin, CW 25, *History of Political Ideas*, vol. 7, *The New Order and Last Orientation*, ed. Jürgen Gebhardt and Thomas A. Hollweck, intro. Jürgen Gebhardt (Columbia: University of Missouri Press, 1999), 175–92; see also esp. the chapters on positivism, Comte, and Marx in Voegelin, CW 26, *History of Political Ideas*, vol. 8, *Crisis and the Apocalypse of Man*, ed. and intro. David Walsh (Columbia: University of Missouri Press, 1999), 88–250, 303–72.

7. For a diagrammatic summary of the results and implications, see the appendix to "Reason: The Classic Experience," in CW 12, *Published Essays*,

and pneumatically, is the chief mark of noetic inquiry and of philosophy as a calling and way of life. The philosopher ineluctably lives the open quest of truth, however, as a *participant* in the In-Between or metaxic common divine-human reality: There is no Archimedean point outside of reality from which to objectively study it, nor is the leap in being or experience of the transcendent Beyond a leap out of the abiding reality of the human condition – a lesson of Plato's Allegory of the Cave.[8] Thus, within the limits of possibility and persuasion, the philosopher is called actively *to resist* untruth through searching noetic critique, grounded as in Aristotle in robust common sense, which is the foundation of prudential rationality and of political science itself.[9] Such resistance

1966–1985, ed. and intro. Ellis Sandoz (Baton Rouge: Louisiana State University Press, 1990), 287–91. For Anaximander and the *apeiron*, see Voegelin, *Order and History*, vol. 2, *The World of the Polis* (Baton Rouge: Louisiana State University Press, 1957), 181–83, and esp. Voegelin, *Order and History*, vol. 4, *The Ecumenic Age* (Baton Rouge: Louisiana State University Press, 1974), 174–92, 215–18.

8. Voegelin, *New Science of Politics*, 79; Voegelin, *Order and History*, vol. 1, *Israel and Revelation* (Baton Rouge: Louisiana State University Press, 1956), 10–11; see Ellis Sandoz, "Voegelin's Philosophy of History and Human Affairs," in *The Politics of Truth and Other Untimely Essays; The Crisis of Civic Consciousness* (Columbia: University of Missouri Press, 1999), chap. 10, §3.

9. As indicated in the text, Voegelin insists on the foundation of political prudential understanding in *common sense* as a mark of the universal rationality displayed in classical philosophy, as that compactly underlies differentiated noesis and provides *zetesis* with its substantive starting points. Thus, he speaks of employing the "Aristotelian procedure" in *The New Science of Politics*, e.g., pp. 34 and 80. The ubiquitous presence of political common sense also is a mark of the *philosophical* superiority of Anglo-American thought to that of Europe, which has been ruined by ideology (ibid., 188–89). See Voegelin, *Autobiographical Reflections*, chap. 10: "American society had a philosophical background far superior in range and existential substance, though not always in articulation, to anything that I found represented in the methodological environment in which I had grown up [in Vienna]" (*CW* 34:57). At the end of *"What Is Political Reality?"* he says, in speaking (to a plenary gathering of the German Association for Political Science in 1965) of Scottish common sense philosophy as given in especially Thomas Reid: "Common sense is a civilizational habit that presupposes noetic experience, without the man of this habit himself possessing differen-

forms against the corruptions of the age at all levels – whether like those of sophistic Athens or of the ideological autonomous men infesting our contemporary existence with fanatical zealotry cloaking *libido dominandi* and the *eros tyrannos* in dreamworld delusions. The traits and detachment from reality of such pneumopathologies were already admirably delineated by Plato in the *Republic* (577c–588a).

The calling and its authoritative consequences are announced, for instance, in Voegelin's essay "The Oxford Political Philosophers." He said: "This is a time [1953] for the philosopher to be aware of his authority, and to assert it, even if that brings him into conflict with an environment infested by dubious ideologies and political theologies – so that the word of Marcus Aurelius will apply to him: 'The philosopher, the priest and servant of the gods.'"[10]

Even more energetically, the transfer of authority from corrupt public institutions to the philosopher is traced in principle as the climax of the *Gorgias,* with plain allusions to his own totalitarian experience: "The man who stands convicted as the accomplice of tyrannical murderers and as the corruptor of his country, does not represent spiritual order, and nobody is obliged to show respect to his word. The authority of public order lies with Socrates. The situation is fascinating for those among us who find ourselves in the Platonic position and who recognize in the men with whom we associate today the intellectual pimps for power who will connive in our murder tomorrow. It would be too much of an honor,

tiated knowledge of noesis. The civilized *homo politicus* need not be a philosopher, but he must have common sense." He continues: "The reference to common sense is meant to make clear once more that, and also why, there can be no 'theory of politics' in terms of fundamental propositions or principles rising above the propositions of an 'empirical' science of politics. For the so-called *empeiria* of politics is the habit of common sense, that although compact, is formed by the *ratio* as the structure [*Sachstruktur*] of consciousness." Voegelin, CW 6, *Anamnesis: On the Theory of History and Politics,* trans. M. J. Hanak and Gerhart Niemeyer, ed. David Walsh (Columbia: University of Missouri Press, 2002), 411.

10. "The Oxford Political Philosophers" in CW 11, *Published Essays, 1953–1965,* ed. and intro. Ellis Sandoz (Columbia: University of Missouri Press, 2000), 46.

however, to burden Callicles personally with the guilt of murder. The whole society is corrupt, and the process of corruption did not start yesterday."[11]

The same applies to Hitler and the Germans, as Voegelin stresses:

> And now we pass to the problematic of crime when the society is not intact, as a problematic that has come to light through the mass murder during the Third Reich. But, as I again and again emphasize, we are speaking, not about the problem of National Socialism, but about Hitler and the Germans. . . . I have continually spoken of moral degeneracy; it does not exist abstractly. . . . It is, rather, a matter of this whole process of intellectual and spiritual degeneration [infecting every level of personal and institutional life with rot]. . . . All of these people are accomplices. I have forgotten nobody – [clergy, judges, generals, professors]. . . . I will not here, for heaven's sake, defend the professors. When in the early 1930s, after Hitler had come into power, a whole series of professors, not only Jews, were relieved of their posts, none of the others . . . ever refused to occupy with pleasure one of the posts vacated through this dismissal. Since I was myself dismissed in 1938, I have always [had] a particularly keen eye for people who became tenured professors in Germany after 1933. So there is this kind of aiding and abetting, one always goes along, there is no one who offers resistance. . . .That does not happen.[12]

3. Truth and Ecumenicity

The language of truth is spoken in many dialects, and no absolute partition between revelation and *noesis* is empirically or theoreti-

11. *Order and History*, vol. 3, *Plato and Aristotle* (Baton Rouge: Louisiana State University Press, 1957), 37–38. For the structure of corruption, see the summary p. 79.
12. *Hitler and the Germans*, CW 31, §43, 230–35.

cally supportable, whatever the institutional differentiations. As Voegelin informed his political science students in Munich from time to time: You can't go back of revelation and pretend it never happened. If apperceptive experience forms the empirical ground of philosophical inquiry and exegesis, then one must attend to insights from that and every other quarter whenever they arise as events of consciousness in concrete individual human beings to form the articulate experiences-symbolizations of noetic exploration. That philosophy by this accounting must be in some sense empirically grounded, and not merely imaginative word-play or logorrhea, however brilliant, if it is to be epistemologically cogent, immediately puts Voegelin at odds with both ideologues devising imaginary second realities (for whom experience is terribly "inconvenient") and much else that otherwise passes for contemporary "autonomous" philosophizing.[13]

That it bridges the distance between pneumatic and noetic discourse to embrace both offends the self-appointed custodians of both revelation and academic philosophy. (So there goes the readership.) Nonetheless, there is this firmly reiterated conclusion:

> We can no longer ignore that the symbols of "Faith" express the responsive quest of man just as much as the revelatory appeal, and that the symbols of "Philosophy" express the revelatory appeal just as much as the responsive quest. We must further acknowledge that the medieval tension between Faith and Reason derives from the origins of these symbols in the two different ethnic cultures of Israel and Hellas, that in the consciousness of Israelite prophets and Hellenic philosophers the differentiating experience of the divine Beyond was respectively focused on the revelatory appeal and the human quest. . . . The reflective action of [Plato and Aristotle] is a

13. Cf., however, David Walsh, "Voegelin's Place in Modern Philosophy," *Modern Age* 49, no. 1 (Winter 2007): 12–23; more fully, David Walsh, *The Modern Philosophical Revolution: The Luminosity of Existence* (Cambridge: Cambridge University Press, 2008).

quest by concrete human beings in response to a divine appeal from the Beyond of the soul.[14]

But it is of utmost importance to grasp that the relationship and process of communion with the divine is not reserved for grandiose personalities. It is the common coin of open existence available to every human being as the precious mark of their humanity as this is confirmed in apperceptive experience. Thus, in noting that reason is "due to God's grace" even according to Aquinas, Voegelin remarks that this understanding applies today and to wherever we may be as well: "You are sitting here asking questions. Why? Because you have that divine *kinesis* in you that moves you to be interested. . . . [I]t is the revelatory presence, of course, that pushes you or pulls you. It's there. We are talking."[15] "The consciousness of being caused by the Divine ground and being in search of the Divine ground – that is reason [*nous*]. Period."[16]

4. Personal Action

At the concrete level of political action, an array of consequences follows that texture the critique of the Nazi period recounted in

14. "The Beginning and the Beyond: A Meditation on Truth," in *CW* 28:211. See the late (1981) summarizing statement on these subjects, entitled "The Meditative Origin of the Philosophical Knowledge of Order," in *CW* 33, *The Drama of Humanity and Other Miscellaneous Papers, 1939–1985*, ed. and intro. William Petropulos and Gilbert Weiss (Columbia: University of Missouri Press, 2004), chap. 14: "In my view there is neither natural reason nor revelation, neither the one nor the other. Rather we have here a theological misconstruction of certain real matters that was carried out in the interest of theological systematization." *CW* 33:385–86.
15. "Conversations with Eric Voegelin," in *CW* 33:243–343, at 328, 330–31. The attitude experientially validates the flux of ubiquitous divine presence in human consciousness implicit in Jesus' promise at the end of the Gospel of Matthew: "[A] nd, lo, I am with you always, even unto the end of the world." Matt. 28:20. On the pushes and pulls (*helkein*) in experiences of divine Reality as recounted in Greek philosophy as well as in biblical revelation, see Voegelin's comparative analysis in "The Gospel and Culture," in *CW* 12:172–212, at 184–91; also "Reason: The Classic Experience," in *CW* 12:265–91, at 281.
16. *CW* 33:329.

Hitler and the Germans and elaborate the cardinal principle energetically asserted in Voegelin's *Antrittsvorlesung,* one that connects the philosopher as a representative figure with every man: "The spiritual disorder of our time, the civilizational crisis of which everyone so readily speaks, does not by any means have to be borne as an inevitable fate; [but], on the contrary, everyone possesses the means of overcoming it is his own life. . . . No one is obliged to take part in the spiritual crisis of a society; on the contrary, everyone is obliged to avoid this folly and live his life in order."[17]

5. Divine-Human Partnership

The transcendent source of order is identified in the first lecture of the course in terms of the immanent present of time and political action as occurring in the "presence under God."[18] "Insofar as . . . man exists under God, he has presence, [which is a problem not just for Germans] but for everyman: to place the immanent present within the immanent process under the judgment of the [divine] presence." It is the calling of the philosopher to utter that judgment and to claim the authority of public order when necessary, for example, under conditions of social schism and disintegration when political and other institutional power and the truth of spirit separate. Thus, as Plato showed in the *Republic* and in the *Gorgias,* "to place oneself under the presence, under the presence of God, and according to that to adjudicate what one does as man and how one forms the order of one's own existence and the existence of society, that for Plato is an act of

17. "Science, Politics and Gnosticism," in *CW* 5, *Modernity Without Restraint,* ed. and intro. Manfred Henningsen (Columbia: University of Missouri Press, 2000), 261.
18. See "Eternal Being in Time" in *CW* 6, *Anamnesis,* chap. 12: "There is no philosophy without philosophers, namely without men whose psychic sensorium responds to eternal being." "The concept most suitable to express the presence of eternal being in the temporal flow is flowing presence." *CW* 6:313 and 329, respectively. See also the discussion in *CW* 33:182–83, 233, 264, 340–41.

judgment. That means that man is always under judgment" – and thus by the logic of the heart persuaded to live his life continuously *sub specie mortis,* under the aspect of death and eternity, as the foundation of the *techne metretike,* or art of measuring basic to political order.[19] As Jürgen Gebhardt comments, in the face of political and spiritual disaster, "it is the philosopher-scholar who is called upon to accept the office of *magisterium* and defend it against intellectual usurpers."[20] A related point is affirmed by Aleksandr Solzhenitsyn: "Then why have literature at all? After all, the writer is a teacher of the people. . . . And a greater writer – forgive me, perhaps I shouldn't say this, I'll lower my voice – a greater writer is, so to speak, a second government. That's why no regime anywhere has ever loved its great writers, only its minor ones."[21]

6. Anthropology and the Tension of Existence

Every human being, Voegelin writes, is *imago Dei* and thereby *called* – a call the individual person in his freedom can respond to, reject, or ignore – to fulfill the promise of his sacred destiny. Thus, man is *theomorphic.* "Through the seeking for the divine, the loving reaching beyond ourselves toward the divine in the philosophical experience and the loving encounter through the Word in the pneumatic experience, man participates in the divine. . . . The specific dignity of man is based on this, on his nature as theomorphic, as in the form and in the image of God. . . . One cannot dedivinize oneself without dehumanizing oneself."[22] "By *spirit* we understand the openness of man to the divine ground of his existence;

---

19. *Hitler and the Germans, CW* 31, §5, p. 71; *Order and History,* vol. 3, *Plato and Aristotle,* 92, 129.
20. Gebhardt in "Vocation of the Scholar," 18, quoted in Ellis Sandoz, *Republicanism, Religion, and the Soul of America* (Columbia: University of Missouri Press, 2006), 180.
21. Solzhenitsyn, *The First Circle,* trans. Thomas P. Whitney (New York: Bantam Books, 1981), 415.
22. *Hitler and the Germans, CW* 31, §8, p. 87.

by *estrangement* from the spirit, the closure and the revolt against the ground. Through spirit man actualizes his potential to partake of the divine. He rises thereby to the *imago Dei* which it is his destiny to be. Spirit in this classical sense of nous, is that which all men have in common, the *xynon* as Heraclitus has called it. Through the life of the spirit, which is common to all, the existence of man becomes existence in community."[23]

7. Spokesmen for Divine Truth

At the conclusion of the lecture on the German university, as we have seen, Voegelin again invoked the words of the prophet Ezekiel as fitting therapy for the pneumopathology of consciousness he has diagnosed and sketched in his meditation on the Nazi disorders. Ultimately, the faithful or responsive human being – whether citizen, soldier, philosopher, priest, or prophet – can do no more than make the public aware of such maladies, as Socrates in the name of truth had done in serving as messenger of God to persuade the Athenians to tend their souls and serve justice. The message is not merely moralistic. It is soteriological and eschatological in content, pertaining to the salvation and destiny of individual human beings, society in history, and the structure-process of reality itself. But its seat is the participatory realm of divine-human consciousness of concrete individual persons. Thus, the saving word reiterated by Voegelin came to Ezekiel from God: "So you, son of man, I have made a watchman for the house of Israel; whenever you hear a word from my mouth, you shall give them warning from me. If I say to the wicked, O wicked man, you shall surely die; and you do not speak to warn the wicked to turn from his way, that wicked man shall die in his iniquity; but his blood I will require at your hand. But if you warn the wicked to turn from his way, and he does not turn from his way, he shall die in his iniquity, but you will have saved your soul." Voegelin told his students

23. "The German University and the Order of German Society: A Reconsideration of the Nazi Era," in *CW* 12:7.

to memorize the passage.[24] As Manfred Henningsen, who was present as one of Voegelin's graduate assistants, writes, the charged atmosphere was that of a "courtroom," with Voegelin the judge. The overall intent of Voegelin in these discourses was to elicit the conversion, or "*metanoia*," of his auditors to truth analogous to that of the denizens in the cave recounted in Plato's *Republic*.[25]

8. Conclusion

At the beginning of his long study of order and history, Voegelin gave a definition: "Philosophy is the love of being through love of divine Being as the source of its order." This enduringly remained the pole star of his life and work.[26]

A consequence of the foregoing discussion is that anybody who is seriously interested in understanding Voegelin as he understood himself is obliged to come to grips with the issues briefly remembered here and clarified textually in numerous places over the decades as artifacts and way stations of the philosopher's own questing meditative life.[27] A second consequence is plainly a substantial, even revolutionary, redefinition of the meaning of

24. Ezek. 33:7–9, quoted as in ibid., 35; earlier quoted to the students with instructions in *Hitler and the Germans,* CW 31:200.

25 Manfred Henningsen, Editor's introduction, *Hitler und die Deutschen,* 29, 38. Cf. *Republic* 518d–e; Voegelin, *Order and History,* vol. 3, *Plato and Aristotle,* 68, 112–17.

26 *Order and History,* vol. 1, *Israel and Revelation,* xiv. See the discussion in Sandoz, *The Voegelinian Revolution,* 141–42.

27. As one astute commentator writes: "It is as if he himself were a second Jeremiah, that Voegelin undertook his own effort to rebalance the consciousness of his own age. . . . His own purpose is clearly one that seeks to recover the prophetic impulse." Geoffrey L. Price, "Recovery from Metastatic Consciousness: Voegelin and Jeremiah," in *Politics, Order and History: Essays on the Work of Eric Voegelin,* ed. Glenn Hughes, Stephen A. McKnight, and Geoffrey L. Price (Sheffield, Eng.: Sheffield Academic Press, 2001), 185–207, at 204. The able editors of *Hitler and the Germans* remark that Voegelin's authoritative appeal for conversion to truth in his auditors is founded as a political philosopher "on his own life of bearing witness" (editors' introductions, CW 31:34).

philosophy itself, especially on the decisive points of (a) underlining the loving tension toward divine Reality in open existence as central, (b) attenuating or abandoning the Scholastic convention separating faith and reason as supernatural and natural, respectively, and (c) discarding as egophany the arrogant pretense of autonomous reason as its originator in self-sufficient human speculators.[28] *The God of Abraham, Moses, Plato, and Paul is one and the same God, disclosed to spiritually sensitive men of all ages and communicated in equivalent language modalities and symbolisms.* To make any other assumption about human communion with divine being would be extraordinary, if one acknowledges that there is one mankind and one reality, of which man is ontologically the self-reflective articulate part.[29] Openness and responsiveness to the luminous presence of ineffable It-reality within limits imposed by metaxic existence is the very essence of what it means to be a human being, on this accounting.[30] More discursively,

28. For discussion of egophany, see Sandoz, *Voegelinian Revolution*, 239–43, and the sources cited therein, esp. Voegelin, *Order and History*, vol. 4, *The Ecumenic Age*, chap. 5, §2, pp. 260–71. For a preliminary elaboration of the revolutionary implications for philosophy per se, see *Voegelinian Revolution*, chap. 7, "*Principia Noetica*: The Voegelinian Revolution – 1981 and Beyond," 189–216. This is a meditative and ontological revolution of mind and spirit, one involving a "change in being," not a political one in the streets, nor even in intractable prevailing climates of opinion, one is constrained to emphasize to help avoid misunderstandings.

29. This is no mere inference; Voegelin is explicit in the matter: "Unless we want to indulge in extraordinary theological assumptions, the God who appeared to philosophers, and who elicited from Parmenides the exclamation 'Is!', was the same God who revealed himself to Moses as the 'I am who (or: what) I am,' as the God who is what he is in the concrete theophany to which man responds. When God lets himself be seen, whether in a burning thornbush or in a Promethean fire, he is what he reveals himself to be in the event" (Voegelin, *Order and History*, vol. 4, *The Ecumenic Age*, chap. 4, §3, p. 229). See also "Equivalences of Experience and Symbolization in History," in *CW* 12:115–33.

30. Some of the implications are discussed in Paul Caringella, "Eric Voegelin: Philosopher of Divine Presence," in *Eric Voegelin's Significance for the Modern Mind*, ed. Ellis Sandoz (Baton Rouge: Louisiana State University Press, 1991), 174–205. Although Voegelin seems never to say so, the ultimate source of the symbol It as used in his work is clearly Pseudo-Dionysius,

Voegelin writes: "Things do not happen in the astrophysical universe; the universe, together with all things founded in it, happens in God."[31] As previously noted, Voegelin later adds that "the questioner's language reveals itself as the paradoxic event of the ineffable becoming effable. . . . In reflective distance, the questioner. . . experiences his speech as the divine silence breaking creatively forth in the imaginative word that will illuminate the quest as the questioner's movement of return to the ineffable silence."[32]

Philosophy, then, is the loving noetic search of the heights and depths of reality conducted as faith seeking understanding and accepting as authoritative truth the insights attained in the open quest of reality experienced: The philosopher is the true type of man.[33] The philosopher thus speaks as the oracle of God in

where the name It represents the ineffable "Super-Essential Godhead which we must not dare . . . to speak, or even to form any conception Thereof, except those things which are divinely revealed to us from the Holy Scriptures." "The Divine Names" 1.2 in *Dionysius the Areopagite: The Divine Names; and The Mystical Theology*, ed, C. E. Rolt (repr.; Kila, MT: Kessinger Publishing, n.d.), 53; see pp. 4–12. N. B.: The presentation here assumes the analysis given in the epilogue to Sandoz, *Voegelinian Revolution*, revised and reprinted in Sandoz, *Republicanism, Religion, and the Soul of America*, chap. 8, "The Spirit of Voegelin's Late Work," esp. pp. 162–81. Behind Thomas's Tetragrammaton stands Dionysius's It, and behind that the *epekeina* (Beyond) of Plato's *agathon* (Good), *kalon* (Beauty), *periechon* (Comprehending), and *to pan* (All) back to Anaximander's *apeiron* (Unbounded, Depth) and similar symbols – matters pertaining to nonexistent reality that must be left aside here. For an analysis of some of the issues, see Voegelin, *Order and History*, vol. 5, *In Search of Order*, ed. Ellis Sandoz (Baton Rouge: Louisiana State University Press, 1987), chap. 2, §11, pp. 100–3; also Fran O'Rourke, *Pseudo-Dionysius and the Metaphysics of Aquinas* (1992; repr. Notre Dame: University of Notre Dame Press, 2005), esp. the section "Aquinas and the Good Beyond Being," exploring the difficulty "of expressing in concepts and terms appropriate to beings that which is supposedly nonexistent, i.e., prime matter, or which is beyond existence, namely, the divine Good" (201).

31. *Order and History*, vol. 4, *The Ecumenic Age*, penultimate page.
32. *Order and History*, vol. 5, *In Search of Order*, 103; see Sandoz, *Voegelinian Revolution*, 264.
33. See *The New Science of Politics* (Chicago: University of Chicago Press, 1952), 63–70. Cf. the fine analysis of Anselm in Robert McMahon, *Understanding the Medieval Meditative Ascent: Augustine, Anselm,*

manifesting receptivity to highest truth[34] – a role of urgent significance when the ordering institutions of a society founder and
abdicate responsibility or collapse and pervert themselves into
instruments of evil, injustice, and murderous destruction, as displayed in lurid detail in Hitler's Germany or Stalin's Russia, but
not only there. And as we have seen, Voegelin reminds all who will
hear of the abiding obligation of every man to live in accordance
with truth and to resist evil and corruption to the limits of their
individual capacities – thereby to serve justice and goodness within possibility, the message of Ezekiel's Watchman. The truth ascertained is neither dogmatic nor exhaustive but existential and self-
augmenting, ecumenic and authoritative, as in accordance with
revelation and reason. To give Voegelin one last word:

> I am indeed attempting to "identify". . . the God who reveals
> himself, not only in the prophets, in Christ, and in the
> Apostles, but wherever his reality is experienced as present in
> the cosmos and in the soul of man. One can no longer use the
> medieval distinction between the theologian's supernatural
> revelation and the philosopher's natural reason, when any
> number of texts will attest the revelatory consciousness of the
> Greek poets and philosophers; nor can one let revelation
> begin with the Israelite and Christian experiences, when the
> mystery of divine presence in reality is attested as experienced
> by man, as far back as 20,000 B.C. . . . As far as my own
> vocabulary is concerned, I am very conscious of not relying
> on the language of doctrine, but I am equally conscious of not
> going beyond the orbit of Christianity when I prefer the expe-

Boethius, and Dante (Washington, DC: Catholic University of America
Press, 2006), esp. 202–10.

34. Although it may at first sight appear to be novel, this is in fact the ordinary
obligation and role of "every man" of faith (not only philosophers,
prophets, and apostles) under the dispensation of Grace as "good stewards
of the manifold grace of God. If any man speak, let him speak as the oracles
of God [_lógia theou_]; if any man minister, let him do it as of the ability which
God gives him: that God may in all things be glorified." 1 Pet. 4:10–11 (KJV
modified).

riential symbol "divine reality" to the God of the Creed, for "divine reality" translates the *theotes* of Colossians 2:9. . . . Moreover, I am very much aware that my inquiry into the history of experience and symbolization generalizes the Anselmian *fides quaerens intellectum* so as to include every *fides,* not only the Christian, in the quest for understanding by reason. . . . In practice this means that one has to recognize, and make intelligible, the presence of Christ in a Babylonian hymn, or a Taoist speculation, or a Platonic dialogue, just as much as in a Gospel.[35]

Perhaps as clearly as any other text, this remarkable statement captures the revolutionary thrust of Voegelin's work. It is a set of claims to be pondered by anyone devoted to the study of order and disorders in human experience in its broadest amplitude, in service to Truth and in resistance against deformation and evil. This is the philosopher's vocation.

Since we are interested in politics, it is well to be reminded of Voegelin's own actions to stem the tide in time and to rectify the effects of the Hitler calamity after the fact – the therapeutic intent of the *Hitler* lectures. He narrowly escaped the Gestapo and fled to Switzerland and the United States in 1938 after the *Anschluss* and being fired from his job as a professor at the University of Vienna, and thus avoided paying the almost certain ultimate price of an opponent of the tyranny. Of his day-to-day activities while a member of the faculty of the University of Vienna in the years leading up to his dismissal by the Nazis, information is meager. His opposition was sufficiently well-known through his publications, however, so that he was regularly identified (in print) as a "Jew." His "mastering of the present,"[36] as he called it in the 1964

35. "Response to Professor Altizer," in *Eric Voegelin's Thought: A Critical Appraisal,* ed. Ellis Sandoz (Durham, NC: Duke University Press, 1982), 190–91; repr. in *CW* 12:292–303, at 294.
36. *Hitler and the Germans, CW* 31, §5, 75. The scarcity of information on the early years is being relieved to some degree through publication of primary materials in Voegelin, *CW* 29, *Selected Correspondence, 1924–1949,* trans. William Petropulos, ed. and intro. Jürgen Gebhardt (Columbia: University

lectures, consisted in publishing three books methodically demon-
strating the fallaciousness and reductionist virulence of National
Socialist pneumopathology – two of them published in 1933 by
German publishers – and condemning it as the apocalypse of evil
and anti-Christianity. As Gregor Sebba later wrote: "When I read
those two books, I knew that Voegelin would be on the Nazi list
when Austria fell. I still wonder how he had the nerve to publish
both books in Hitler's Germany, and how two German publishers
could accept them."[37] The third of these took as its epigraph a line

of Missouri Press, 2009); cf. Sandoz, *Voegelinian Revolution*, chap. 2; also
Cooper, *Eric Voegelin and the Foundations of Modern Political Science*,
chap. 1. In terms of chronology, the *Anschluss* annexing Austria to the Third
Reich occurred with the arrival of German troops in Vienna on March 11,
1938; Voegelin was fired by the university on April 23; he escaped to Zurich
on July 14; and he departed with Lissy from Paris for America on September
8, 1938. Cf. Monika Puhl, *Eric Voegelin in Baton Rouge* (Munich: Wilhelm
Fink Verlag, 2005), 20–21. The chilling letter of dismissal reads as follows
(trans. William Petropulos as in *CW 29*):

University of Vienna: Faculty of Law and Staatswissenschaft [Political
Science]
Vienna, April 23, 1938
To Associate Professor Dr. Erich Voegelin, Vienna.

> As Temporary Dean of the Faculty of Law and Staatswissenschaft it is my
> official duty to inform you that, with the decree of April 22, 1938,
> Zl.10606-I-le, the Austrian Ministry of Education has cancelled its certi-
> fication of the right to lecture that was previously granted to you, and
> thereby revokes its authorization for you to teach. Therefore, pending
> further notice, you are to abstain from the exercise of any and all teach-
> ing activities, and any other activities which may fall within the wider
> purview of your previously held position.

Heil Hitler!
The Temporary Dean of the Faculty of Law and Staatswissenschaft
37. Translated as *Race and State* (CW 2; Baton Rouge: Louisiana State
University Press, 1997) and *The History of the Race Idea: From Ray to
Carus* (CW 3; Baton Rouge: Louisiana State University Press, 1998), both
trans. Ruth Hein and ed. Klaus Vondung. Gregor Sebba was Voegelin's col-
league and friend in Vienna, later professor at Emory University, quoted
from "Prelude and Variations on the Theme of Eric Voegelin" in *Eric
Voegelin's Thought*, 3-65 at 11. Hannah Arendt regarded *Race and State* as
"the best historical account of race-thinking." Arendt, *Origins of
Totalitarianism* (New York: Harcourt, Brace and Co., 1951), 158n.

from Dante's *Inferno* (canto 3, line 1): "Per me si va ne la città dolente"[38] (Through me the way is to the City of Woe). The earthly hell was at hand. As for Voegelin himself, there was no chariot of fire translating him to heaven as for Elijah, only the evening train to Zurich after a day spent eluding the Gestapo in Vienna, on the way to a new life in America, trembling as he went.[39]

Most of Voegelin's major work lay ahead. Twenty years after the abrupt departure from Vienna, he returned to Munich, partly motivated by the hope of instilling "the spirit of American democracy" into Germany and of "injecting an element of international consciousness, and of democratic attitudes, into German political science."[40]

---

38. Translated as *The Political Religions* in *CW 5, Modernity Without Restraint*, ed. and intro. Manfred Henningsen (Columbia: University of Missouri Press, 2000), 19–73 at 20.
39. See *Autobiographical Reflections*, CW 34:1–148, at 71, 82–83.
40. Ibid., 116.

9. Conclusion: The Politics of Liberty

Give me Liberty or give me death is the famous cry of Patrick Henry. As he stated it on March 23, 1775: "Is life so dear, or peace so sweet, as to be purchased at the price of chains and slavery? Forbid it, Almighty God! I know not what course others may take; but as for me, give me liberty or give me death!"[1] The *Liberty* he proclaimed he and his contemporaries understood to be a gift of the Almighty to human beings in their individual existences as unique personalities, each one created in the image and likeness of God and, thus, *imago Dei*. The whole of our civilization, back to the Exodus three-and-a-half millennia ago of the Hebrew people, long held captive in Egypt, and memorialized in the Passover, is built around this understanding. Its meaning and consequences have formed the substance of the little book you hold in your hands and which I now conclude.

Although we properly begin in the middle, the *Liberty* we prize reaches the heights and depths of reality as humanly experienced, from the transcendent divine down to the material foundations of the hierarchy of being constitutive of existence – as we have observed in foregoing pages and as invoked in Patrick Henry's own statement, where he appeals not merely to reason but to "experience." The antonyms of Liberty so conceived are *slavery* and *tyranny*. Their remediation is to resist evil and to live free of physical as well as intellectual bondage in accordance with Truth. This is Patrick Henry's line of argument and context. He gives voice to views representative of the vision of reality invoked in revelation and in philosophy as well as in the American Founders' interpretation of the traditional political and constitutional order then under deadly assault. This vision found numerous complementary

1. U.S. Historical Documents, www.law.ou.edu.

statements throughout the period, all well summarized in Thomas Jefferson's motto: Resistance to tyrants is obedience to God.[2]

This was a potent theme in the discourse of the period. The liberty claimed through Christ is freedom from the law and the gift of righteousness through divine Grace, as powerfully evoked in Paul's Epistle to the Galatians, culminating in: "So then, brethren, we are not children of the bondwoman, but of the free. Stand fast therefore in the liberty wherewith Christ hath made us free, and be not entangled again with the yoke of bondage" (Gal. 4:31–5:1). During the Great Awakening, Elisha Williams had quoted these verses in his *The Essential Rights and Liberties of Protestants"* (1744) and added: "Where the Spirit of the Lord is, there is Liberty" (2 Cor. 3:17). He wrote: "It is impossible to suppose that God by his special Grace in the gospel should free us from the bondage of ceremonies, [and] his own command-ments . . . and [then] subject us to a more grievous yoke, the commandments of men. . . . 'You are called to Liberty,' Gal. 5:13. I Cor. 7:23: 'Be not ye the Servants of Men . . . ,' a com-mand accompan'd with the weightiest reasons. Rom. 14:9, 10: 'For to this End Christ both died and rose and revived; that he might be Lord, both of the Dead and Living.'"[3] In the year the Constitution was framed, Nathanael Emmons preached on *The Dignity of Man*. A leader of the New Divinity, and taking Solomon as his paradigm, he began with philosophical anthro-pology and reminded his auditors:

> The dignity of man appears from his bearing the image of his Maker. . . . This allows us to say, that man is the offspring of

2. For illustration and discussion see Ellis Sandoz, *A Government of Laws: Political Theory, Religion, and the American Founding* (1990; repr. Columbia: University of Missouri Press, 2001), 140–60; also Ellis Sandoz, *The Politics of Truth and Other Untimely Essays: The Crisis of Civic Consciousness* (Columbia: University of Missouri Press, 1999), 204n6.

3. Philalethes [Elisha Williams], *The Essential Rights and Liberties of Protestants* (Boston, 1744), in *Political Sermons of the American Founding Era, 1730–1805*, ed. Ellis Sandoz, 2nd ed., 2 vols. (1991; repr. Indianapolis: Liberty Fund, 1998), 1:51–118, at 85–86.

God, a ray from the fountain of light, a drop from the ocean of intelligence. . . . His soul is a transcript of the natural perfections of the Deity. God is a spirit, and so is the soul of man; God is intelligence and activity, and so is the soul of man. In a word, man is the living image of the living God, in whom is displayed more of the divine nature and glory, than in all the works and creatures of God upon earth. Agreeably therefore to the dignity of his nature, God hath placed him at the head of the world, and given him the dominion over his works. Hence says the Psalmist [Ps. 8], "Thou has made him a little lower than the angels, and hast crowned him with glory and honour. Thou has madest him to have dominion over the works of thy hands; thou has put all things under his feet . . ." How wide is the kingdom of man! How numerous his subjects! How great his dignity.[4]

This appeal to the individual conscience is accompanied by the sense of civic responsibility for just dominion that makes the safety and well-being of the community (*salus populi*) the supreme law and liberty under law the highest good of the community, to remember John Selden as he was invoked in the debate over American liberty.[5] In the context of constitutionalism, the notion of "No taxation without representation" proclaimed an enduring theme, as Edmund Burke stressed in his *Speech on Conciliation* of March 15, 1775: The Americans are descendants of Englishmen, he reminded the House of Commons. "They are therefore not

4. Nathanael Emmons, *The Dignity of Man* [Providence 1787], in *Political Sermons*, ed. Sandoz, 1:883–907, at 887–88. The appeal to Solomon as paradigmatic, along with Emmons's evident confidence in scientific progress, hints at Sir Francis Bacon's fantasy "New Atlantis" and and Salomon's House as its guiding institution. For this material, see Francis Bacon, *New Atlantis and The Great Instauration* [1626 and 1620], rev. ed., ed. Jerry Weinberger (Wheeling, IL: Harlan Davidson, 1989).
5. For Selden's words, see Johnson, Cole, et al., eds., *Proceedings in Parliament*, 1628, 2:183, i.e.: *Salus populi suprema lex, et libertas popula summa salus populi*. For details, see Paul Christianson, *Discourse on History, Law, and Governance in the Public Career of John Selden, 1610–1635* (Toronto: University of Toronto Press, 1996), chap. 2.

only devoted to liberty, but to liberty according to English ideas and on English principles. Abstract liberty, like other mere abstractions, is not to be found. Liberty inheres in some sensible object; and every nation has formed itself some favorite point, which by way of eminence becomes the criterion of their happiness. It happened . . . that the great contests for freedom in this country were from the earliest times chiefly upon the question of taxing."[6] From Magna Carta to the Commerce clause in the U.S. Constitution and the contemporary conflict over "ObamaCare," the struggle for liberty still intimately relates to the question of taxing.[7] Whoever controls the money and private property controls the man whose it is as well. From the perspective of the Founders, John Witherspoon – James Madison's professor at Princeton and the only clergyman to sign the Declaration of Independence – wrote powerfully regarding the connection between personal liberty and property: "There is not a single instance in history in which civil liberty was lost, and religious liberty preserved entire. If therefore we yield up our temporal property, we at the same time deliver the conscience into bondage."[8]

Ontology, philosophical anthropology, and politics, as Voegelin demonstrated in earlier pages of this book, all converge in the lives of individual persons and in the peculiar challenges to truth and justice emergent in political history in the turbulent course of events. As noticed earlier, the individual human being is the intersection of time and eternity. He lives not only in the present but in the Presence of God and is thus under judgment. The universal is nowhere encountered except in particulars. The American politics of *resistance* to tyranny is cast in universal terms

6. Peter J. Stanlis, ed., *Edmund Burke: Selected Writings and Speeches* (Chicago: Regnery, 1963), 158.
7. Cases decided by the U.S. Supreme Court in July 2012, The Affordable Care Act Cases, 567 U.S. _____ 2012, pagination pending publication.
8. *Works of the Reverend John Witherspoon*, ed. John Rodgers, 4 vols. (Philadelphia: W.W. Woodward, 1800–1801), 3:37. On Witherspoon more generally, see Scott Philip Segrest, *America and the Political Philosophy of Common Sense* (Columbia: University of Missouri Press, 2010), chap. 3 and passim.

in the Declaration of Independence and elsewhere because the events and experiences are taken to be representative of universal mankind and of the participatory human condition itself as experienced in the metaxy. They exemplify universal principles grounded in nature and in the transcendent order of being. Thus, "All men are created equal and are endowed by their Creator with certain unalienable rights." This also is why political science is a *philosophical*, not a natural, science and why the reductionist fads ruling inquiry in the field of late are inadequate to the noble purposes they ostensibly serve.[9] The American Founders were not confused on the point, even if much of today's academy in anti-spiritualist rebellion remains doggedly oblivious to fundamental issues.

The American resistance and founding conserved a unique and stirring constitutional tradition and civic consciousness. It was enlivened by the force of the Great Awakening from the 1730s onward, then focused and intensified by the fierce power of the debate over the Stamp and Declaratory acts down to the Declaration – a period of two decades producing a veritable school of Liberty, one that created a distinctively American civic consciousness in the process.[10] What they concluded after the framing of the Constitution was brilliantly summarized by Israel Evans in 1791:

> I will endeavour to shew when it may be said that a people *stand fast in the liberty wherewith they are free*. . . . The people are in the habit and exercise of liberty, when they resort

9. For elaboration see chaps. 6–8 herein and Ellis Sandoz, *The Voegelinian Revolution: A Biographical Introduction*, 2nd ed. (1981; repr. New Brunswick: Transaction Pubs., 2000), chap. 7, "*Principia Noetica*: The Voegelinian Revolution – 1981 and Beyond." For those persons slow to grasp the argument here, I can only say with New York's Mayor Koch, "I can explain it for you, but I can't comprehend it for you." A major recent effort in explanation is Brendan Purcell, *From Big Bang to Big Mystery: Human Origins in the Light of Creation and Evolution* (Dublin: Veritas Publications, 2011), esp. pt. 2, pp. 76–143.

10. See Ellis Sandoz, "The Crisis of Civic Consciousness: Nihilism and Resistance," in *The Politics of Truth and Other Untimely Essays*, (Columbia: University of Missouri Press, 1999), chap. 8, 121–38.

to the first principles of government, and trace their rights up to God the Creator: when they exercise their natural power of framing any social compact conducive to the common interest: feel independent of all human power but that which flows from themselves: disdain the subjection of their consciences to any authority but the will of God: refuse to be controuled by the will of any man who claims an independent power of disposing of their lives and estates: recollect that they entered into society to have their natural rights, which are the basis of civil rights, secured. To maintain such principles of original justice, is to stand fast in the righteous liberty of man. True liberty suffers no man to be injured in his person, estate, or character: it encourages and enables him to improve his happiness; and, within the limits of the public good, insures to him every blessing to which imperfect human nature can attain. All the toils, sufferings, treasure and blood of men, are not lost, when they are the price and purchase of liberty. Without religious and civil liberty, we can have no security of life, or of any of the good things of God: we cannot practice the sentiments of our consciences: but where the rights of man are equally secured in the greatest degree, there is the greatest happiness – *and that is our country.*[11]

As Evans's statement suggests, the Patriots drew on resources going back especially to the previous century and to the struggle against Stuart claims to divine right absolutism. Thus, John Milton fervently wrote of the *Liberty* lying at the heart of our vision of the free individual human being, created *imago Dei,* and of the free government most conducive to human flourishing, saying in one place:

11. Israel Evans, "*Sermon delivered at Concord . . .*(1791)," in *Political Sermons*, ed. Sandoz, 2:1059–80, at 1068. For a large collection of related material, see Charles S. Hyneman and Donald S. Lutz, eds., *American Political Writing during the Founding Era, 1760–1805*, 2 vols. (Indianapolis: Liberty Fund, 1983). For the constitutional background in brief, see John Phillip Reid, *The Ancient Constitution and the Origins of Anglo-American Liberty* (DeKalb: Northern Illinois University Press, 2005).

Know that to be *free* is precisely the same thing as to be pious, wise, just and temperate, careful of one's own, abstinent from what is another's, and thence, in fine, magnanimous and brave – so, to be the opposite of these, is the same thing as to be a slave. . . . If it be hard, if it be against the grain, to be slaves, learn to obey right reason, to be masters of yourselves. . . . Unless you do this to the utmost of your power, you will be thought neither by God nor man . . .to be fit persons in whose hands to leave liberty [and] the government of the commonwealth.[12]

Another major voice was that of Algernon Sidney, who gave his life on the scaffold for the *Good Old Cause* (d. 1683) and who thought, "God helps those who help themselves" – and we remember him for saying it.[13] Sidney argued that

If governments arise from the consent of men, and are instituted by men according to their own inclinations, they did therein seek their own good; for the will is ever drawn to some good, or the appearance of it. This is that which [each] man seeks by all the regular or irregular motions of his mind. Reason and passion, virtue and vice, do herein concur. . . . A people, therefore, [who set up any government do it] . . .that it may be well with themselves and their posterity.[14]

Thereby Sidney recapitulates Aquinas's philosophy of natural law.[15]

Finally it should be noted that *egalitarianism* in America – and democratization as it grew in the period leading up to independence

12. John Milton, *Second Defence of the People of England*, in *Areopagitica and Other Political Writings of John Milton*, ed. John Alvis (Indianapolis: Liberty Fund, 1999), 412.
13. Algernon Sidney, *Discourses Concerning Government*, ed. Thomas G. West (Indianapolis: Liberty Fund, 1996), 210.
14. Ibid., 49.
15. Cf. *Summa theologica* I–II, q.94, a.2, in *The Political Ideas of St. Thomas Aquinas: Representative Selections*, ed. Dino Bigongiari (New York: Hafner, 1969), 44–46.

– is not that of the revolutions of the miserable, as Hannah Arendt has called them.[16] Rather, it strongly partakes of common sense as well as of an extraordinary aristocratic sentiment sounded centuries before in the writings of the so-called Norman Anonymous in the *York Tractates* (ca. 1100). He saw every individual as theomorphic, carrying the image of God in himself, standing in immediacy to God (1 Pet. 2:9),[17] and elevating the common man, when a baptized believer, to king and priest as a son of the heavenly *Rex et sacerdos*: "He who puts on Christ in baptism, assumes His royal sacerdotal nature [and is] reborn."[18] This understanding in a Bible-reading society of the individual person as Christ-bearing, his defining attribute being that he is *capable of God* (as the judicious Hooker and John Wesley stressed),[19] rather than merely rational, echoed

16. Hannah Arendt. *On Revolution* (1963; repr. London: Penguin Books, 1990), 94–95, 113–14.
17. "But ye are a chosen generation, a royal priesthood, an holy nation, a peculiar people: that ye should shew forth the praises of him who hath called you out of darkness into his marvelous light: which in time past *were* not a people, but *are* now the people of God: which had not obtained mercy, but now have obtained mercy." 1 Pet. 2:9–10; cf. Rev. 1:6 (KJV).
18. George Huntston Williams, *The Norman Anonymous of 1100 A.D.*, Harvard Theological Studies 18 (Cambridge, MA: Harvard University Press, 1951), 143–44, incorporating n476.
19. Thus Hooker writes: "Complete union with Him must be according unto every power and faculty of our minds apt to receive so glorious an object. Capable we are of God both by understanding and will, by understanding as he is sovereign truth, which comprehendeth the rich treasures of all wisdom; by will, as he is that sea of goodness, whereof whoso tasteth shall thirst no more. . . . Man doth seek a triple perfection, first, a sensual . . . then an intellectual, consisting in those things which none underneath man is either capable of or acquainted with; lastly a spiritual and divine, consisting in those things whereunto we tend by supernatural means here, but cannot attain unto them. . . . That there is somewhat higher than either of these [first] two no other proof doth need, than the very process of man's desire . . . yea, somewhat above capacity of reason, somewhat divine and heavenly, which with hidden exultation it rather surmiseth than conceiveth; somewhat it seeketh and what that is directly it knoweth not, yet very intentive desire thereof doth so incite it, that all other known delights and pleasures are laid aside, they give place to the search for this but only suspected desire. . . . For although the beauties, riches, honours, sciences, virtues, and perfections of all men living were in the present possession of

through the sermons and hymns in America. It reinforced the core notion of the Gospel: "Inasmuch as ye have done *it* unto one of the least of these my brethren, ye have done it unto me" (Matt. 25:40), thereby invoking the presence of Christ in everyman. Every man a king? The principle is there, and it is propagated from the time of the Norman Anonymous to John Wycliffe and then, much later, with vigor by the evangelists including John Leland, Madison's fiery constituent.[20] In this country *We the People* are king, as the principle of popular sovereignty routinely teaches. More than this, however, is the attribution of aristocracy of mind, soul, and character to the "poor in spirit" (Matt. 5:3) – thereby inverting the world's assessment of individuals and God's judgment of them by laying the spiritual foundation for human dignity and its indelible presence in every single man and woman, even the lowly and despised. Leland thundered: "Has God chosen many of the wise and learned? Has he not hidden the mystery of gospel truth from them and revealed it unto babes? . . . Is not a simple man, who makes nature and reason his study a competent judge of things? Is the Bible written (like Caligula's laws) so intricate and high that none but the letter-learned (according to the common phrase) can read it? Is not the vision written so plain that he that runs may read it?"[21] Samuel Miller in New York summarized the case in 1793 by arguing that

> the prevalence of real Christianity, tends to promote the principles and love of political freedom. . . . It contemplates the happiness of the community, as the primary object of all

one: yet somewhat beyond and above all this there would still be sought and earnestly thirsted for." Richard Hooker, *Of the Laws of Ecclesiastical Polity*, ed. A. S. McGrade, Cambridge Texts in the History of Political Thought (Cambridge: Cambridge University Press, 1989), i.ii.3–4, pp.102–4. For John Wesley, see his sermon *The General Deliverance* (1782), sermon no. 60 in *The Works of John Wesley*, vol. 2, *Sermons II*, ed. Albert C. Outler (Nashville: Abingdon Press, 1984), 438–39, and the discussion in Sandoz, *Republicanism, Religion, and the Soul of America* (Columbia: University of Missouri Press, 2006), §5, pp 17–37.

20. Cf. John Leland, *The Rights of Conscience Inalienable* [Boston, 1791], in *Political Sermons*, ed. Sandoz, 2:1079–99.

21. Ibid., 2:1090.

political associations – and it teaches those, who are placed at the helm of government, to remember, that they are called to preside over equals and friends, whose best interest, and not the demands of selfishness, is to be the object of their first and highest care. . . . It forbids us to call, or to acknowledge, any one master upon earth, knowing that we have a Master in heaven, to whom both rulers, and those whom they govern, are equally accountable. In a word, Christianity, by illuminating the minds of men, leads them to consider themselves, as they really are, all co-ordinate terrestrial princes, stripped, indeed, of the empty pageantry and title, but retaining the substance of dignity and power.[22]

Eternal vigilance is the price of Liberty, we are told, and there is no reason to doubt it. The tension of freedom with ever-lurking servitude and tyranny haunts free government and free men as an omnipresent and insidious threat. The great receding totalitarian tyranny of recent memory (the cloven hoof of modernity), exemplified by Hitler and Stalin and Mao, finds a parade of epigones on left and right. They all prosper in the bleak intellectual horizon of a lost metaphysical certainty supplanted by urbane materialistic derision or by a flaccid political correctness unable to analyze murderous dogmatic jihadism for the lethal threat it is for fear of being judgmental. Befuddled silence prevails even when the Hausas' Boko Haram (the group's name means "sin of Western education"), for instance, obstructs gifted Nigerian students from returning home again for fear of being assassinated upon arrival. There is no shortage of threats. Nor are they all external. The appeal to transcendent divinity as revealed in Christianity, the theoretical and historical backbone of the American stance and civilization, has grown woefully out of favor with the self-anointed elite. Of course, solace can and must be taken from the consideration that the divine order of being itself is left untouched by human defections. It matters not whether they are ostentatious, as

22. Samuel Miller, *A Sermon, Preached in New York, July 4th, 1793 . . .* , ibid., 2:1151–67 at 1157.

in the Death of God movements, or more ingratiating and addictive as in the "soft despotism" of statism and social do-good-ism, like soma being freely distributed through sundry new community action and welfare society programs.[23] In Voegelin's trenchant formulation:

> Yet even if the life of the spirit sinks to the level of enlightened reason, to bourgeois morality, and to liberal or nonliberal *Weltanschauungen*, and even if the symbols of transcendence are subjected to serious deformations of their meaning and become discredited, nevertheless these occurrences leave the order of being itself utterly unchanged. Even if Hegel, Marx, and Nietzsche thoroughly murder God and explain him away as dead, divine being remains eternal and man must still get on with living his life sealed by his creatureliness and by death. When concupiscent fantasy shifts the accents of reality, it then imposes a false image on reality. We speak of this fantasy image as the *second reality*. And when man tries to live in this second reality, when he attempts to transform himself from the *imago Dei* into an *imago hominis*, then conflicts arise with the first reality, whose order continually exists.[24]

23. Cf. Paul A. Rahe, *Soft Despotism, Democracy's Drift: Montesquieu, Rousseau, Tocqueville and the Modern Prospect* (New Haven: Yale University Press, 2009). For this "particular form of tyranny, called democratic despotism" in its modern guise, see Tocqueville's summary in Alexis de Tocqueville, *The Ancien Régime and the French Revolution*, trans. Gerald Bevan, intro. Hugh Brogan (London: Penguin Books, 2008): "They undertook . . . to mould together a centralized administration without bounds and a dominant legislative body – administration by bureaucrats and government by voters" (164, 166). Then there is Huxley: "The dedicated *soma* tablets were placed in the centre of the table. The loving cup of strawberry ice cream *soma* was passed from hand to hand. . . . The *soma* had begun to work. Eyes shone, cheeks were flushed, the inner light of universal benevolence broke out on every face in happy, friendly smiles." Aldous Huxley, *Brave New World* (1932; repr. New York: Harper Perennial Modern Classics, 2006), 80–81.

24. Voegelin, *CW* 31, *Hitler and the Germans*, trans., ed., and intro. Detlev Clemens and Brendan Purcell (Columbia: University of Missouri Press, 1999), 262.

This analysis sternly reminds us that the order of being is not at the beck and call of every yahoo sophist who comes along glibly clamoring for power and gratification of his *libido dominandi* through mendacity, guile, and gaming the system. The founding generation resisted corruption with all the civilizational resources available from Aristotle, Cicero, and education in classical philosophy more generally; biblical faith experientially and theoretically grounded; a solid common law constitutional heritage refined by decades of self-government and prudential habit; and by Enlightenment optimism and confidence in the individual human being and the open horizon of human existence reaching upward toward the transcendent and forward toward a better world for all human beings. They were resilient, hopeful, and realistic. The tawdry lures of materialist reductionism and the eschatological politics of utopian dreamers – so in vogue even today – largely fell on deaf ears because of solid experience and common sense as well as stable institutions and civic consciousness attuned to the truth of differentiated reality and devoted to *salus populi*. This complex amalgam constituted the *politics of Liberty*, as I have tried to show. This settled outlook of conviction was, indeed, standing fast in the Liberty wherewith Christ had made them free – as they believed and sought to live it. It was the formative ground for decrying corruption in England and for resisting tyranny in America to the point of death. All of this mattered then, and it still matters now. As Arnold Toynbee demonstrated in his great *A Study of History*, every civilization known to mankind has disintegrated because of internal rot and collapse, and the symptoms are evident in America.[25] In his early study of the German debacle as it brought Hitler and National Socialism to power, Voegelin saw religious revival as the ultimate prophylaxis to counter satanic evil in German society. He concluded that when faced with

> the existence of a substance that is not only morally bad but
> also religiously evil and satanic . . . it can only be resisted by

25. Cf. Arnold J. Toynbee, *A Study of History*, 12 vols. (Oxford: Oxford University Press, 1934–61), esp. vol. 9 [1954], *The Prospects of Western Civilization*, 406–640.

an equally strong religious force of good. One cannot combat a satanic force with morality and humanity alone. However, this difficulty cannot be remedied by simple resolve. Today, no major thinker in the Western world is unaware . . . that the world is undergoing a severe crisis, a process of withering, which has its origin in the secularization of the spirit and . . . severance of a consequently purely secular spirit from its religious roots. No major thinker is ignorant of the fact that recovery can only be brought about by religious renewal, whether within the framework of the Christian churches or outside it. A significant renewal can proceed only from great religious personalities, but it is possible for everyone to prepare himself and to do what he can to prepare the ground in which resistance to evil may grow. It is precisely in this respect that the politicizing intellectuals fail completely.[26]

So what is left? For our generation to take heart anew; patiently to proclaim *truth,* as far as we can discern it, and nurture its abiding transcendental presence; to persuade fellow citizens of it; individually to resist by every means the plunge into the abyss to the limits of our personal capacities as beings capable of God; and last, to join the enduring remnant whose defiant yet hopeful watchword first sounded millennia ago to repudiate the idolatries (or second realities) of that distant age in Joshua's sober cry, "As for me and my house, we will serve the Lord," and reverberates still in Paul's mighty exhortation to "Stand fast therefore in the Liberty wherewith Christ hath made us Free."[27]

To give one of the greatest of the Founders the last word, let us not succumb to the blandishments of *Realpolitik,* which excuses every excess up to and including even atrocity. Rather, John Adams sounded the sobering alarm in his day – and it still rever-

26. Eric Voegelin, "Foreword to the Second Edition of *The Political Religions,*" in *CW 33, The Drama of Humanity and Other Miscellaneous Papers, 1939–1985,* ed. and intro. William Petropulos and Gilbert Weiss (Columbia: University of Missouri Press, 2004), 22–23.
27. Josh. 24:15 and Gal. 5:1 (KJV).

berates down to our own – to give substance to "eternal vigilance":

> Let us see delineated before us the *true map of man*. Let us hear the dignity of his nature, and the noble rank he holds among the works of God – . . . that God Almighty has promulgated from heaven, liberty, peace and good will to man! . . . The prospect now before us in America . . . ought to engage the attention of every man of learning to matters of power and of right, that we may be neither led nor driven blindfolded to irretrievable destruction. . . . There seems to be a direct and formal design on foot to enslave all America. This, however, [can only] be done by degrees.[28]

---

28. *The Political Writings of John Adams: Representative Selections*, ed. George A. Peek Jr. (Indianapolis and New York: Bobbs-Merrill Co., 1954), 19–20, italics added.

Index

Index

Anthropological principle, 6. *See also* Human nature

Antrittsvorlesung, 86

Apeiron (unbounded, depth), 6, 64n18, 80, 91n30

Apology (Plato), 119

Apostles' Creed, 25

Aquinas, Saint Thomas: consciousness of, 6; as first Whig, 3, 43; and Founding Fathers, 43; on Good beyond being, 91n30; on grace, 85; on human nature, 8, 9–10, 12–13; on love, 12–13; as mystic, 59n4; on natural law, 42; and natural law, 3, 102; on Tetragrammaton, 91n30; on unjust law, 42, 42n5

Arendt, Hannah, 10, 94n37, 103

Arete (excellence), 7

Aristotle: civilizational resources available from, 107; connection between divine *pneuma* and, 74; and Founding Fathers, 22, 31, 43, 45; grounding of, in common sense, 81, 81n9; on happiness, 28; on *homonoia* (concord), 11, 16–17, 21, 21n1; on human nature, 16, 24–25; on immortalizing, 7, 28–29; as influence on Voegelin, 78, 79; on liberty versus tyranny, 41; on *nomos* (law), 25, 31n21; on *nous* (reason), 25; on *philia*, 29; on *phronimos*, 45; on political nature of humans, 10, 11, 17, 21; on private property, 14; on virtuous life, 7, 19. *See also specific works*

Aspiration: to the Good, 12–13; politics of, 11–15

Atheist humanists, 35

Atomic bombs, 52

Augustine, Saint: on *amor Dei*, 29; consciousness of, 6; on human destiny, 9; on *imago Dei* (image of God), 8; as mystic, 71; on pursuit of transcendent Good, 13; on soul, 73, 76; on unjust law, 19, 42, 42n5; and *via negativa*, 57; Western politics after, 24

Austin, John, 43

Austria, 93, 94, 94n36. *See also* University of Vienna

Authoritarian State, The (Voegelin), 80n6

Autobiographical Reflections (Voegelin), 64n19, 70, 80n6, 81n9, 95n39

Averroists, 58

Bagehot, Walter, 53

Baptism, 103

Baptists, 25, 37

Baumgarten, Eduard, 74n9

Bay of Pigs, 48

"Beginning and the Beyond, The" (Voegelin), 85n14

Being. *See* Ground of being; Hierarchy of being; Leap in being

Bergson, Henri, 11n12, 65

Beyond, 66, 78n4, 81, 84–85, 91n30

Bible, 5, 9, 25, 34, 103–4, 107. *See also specific books of the Bible*

Bigongiari, Dino, 42n5, 102n15

Bill of Rights, U.S. Constitution, 3, 37, 44

Billings, John, 13–14

Biologism, 71